Forget What You Know About Strategy:

The Hazards of Strategic Planning

Robert Aguilar

First Forecast Press
ISBN# Paperback: 979-8-9904254-1-5
ISBN# eBook: 979-8-9904254-0-8

CONTENTS

To my wife, Rachelle, and my two daughters, Reagan and Roslynn, and to my friends and family who inspire me to become a better version of myself every day. Thank you all for your love and support.

INTRODUCTION

WHY READ THIS BOOK?

Quite simply, my calling is to contribute to the betterment of organizations.

I've spent over half of my life in the bowels of organizational life, and I've worked countless hours—often well into the night—to help bring about positive change.

While some efforts inevitably failed, others met varying levels of success. But all the while, I took notes, learned from the scars that were inflicted along the way, and made the commitment early on to take those experiences and forge a better way to improve organizational conditions. My mission is to help senior leaders and employees—at all levels—make their place of business better and to improve the livelihoods, and thereby lives, of workers like me who spend the greater portions of our lives in these organizations.

For so many of us, the organizations of which we are a part take on a significant relevance to multiple aspects of our life, and the people with whom we work become an extended part of our family. Having had this perspective early on, I did everything I could to learn about organizational life and to contribute to positive change. I launched a concerted effort at acquiring all of the tools I knew would help me navigate my course in leadership, strategic decision-making, and analytical and economic frameworks.

I embarked on my adventure in my late teens by enrolling in Air Force ROTC officer training, where I was formally taught how to take action and lead teams of people. This would result in earning my commission in the US Air Force. In parallel, I studied economics/ econometrics and business leadership as an undergraduate.

After completing my tenure as an undergraduate and ROTC cadet, I entered the US Air Force as an active duty Air Force officer. I spent the next several years serving in various leadership roles at the crossroads of senior leaders, rank-and-file staff, and trends in the external environment. I pursued formal certifications in project, program, and portfolio management, devoured books on strategy and leadership, and earned an MBA from a top business school.

What I've learned over the course of my career can be boiled down to one pivotal takeaway: The classic approach to strategy will not yield the results you need to catapult your company into the vision of what it could become tomorrow. The dynamic, technology-driven, economic whipsaw that characterizes today's landscape requires a completely alternative strategic planning paradigm than what was true even just a handful of years ago.

So forget what you thought you knew about strategy. Fasten your seat belt. We're going to go where most strategic plans fear to tread.

CHAPTER ONE

STRATEGY IS USELESS

Is Your Company on Autopilot?

Forbes recently reported that in today's fast-paced and ever-changing business climate, the company is no longer at the helm. Consumers and employees are the ones that dictate what the future sight picture will look like.[1]

Too many companies do one of two things: They fail to plan and remain in cruise control or they plan to fail by taking too long to develop and execute the perfect plan. Both scenarios lead to disillusionment and apathy, since employees see how unresponsive these approaches are to shifting market conditions.

> *Too many companies do one of two things: They fail to plan and remain in cruise control or they plan to fail by taking too long to develop and execute the perfect plan.*

If you think you're immune to this syndrome, you might want to think again. Eighty-eight percent of Fortune 500 firms that were once thriving, ardent businesses in the 1950s are now off the map. A perfect example of this is the former video rental giant, Blockbuster Video. At one time, this rental services colossus employed more than

80,000 people and operated over 9,000 locations worldwide. However, Blockbuster refused to keep pace with the tidal wave of digitization and quickly began to lose sales in 2004. By 2010, after the CEO had refused an offer from the nascent and burgeoning Netflix to be bought for $50 million, Blockbuster's demise was sealed. The company filed for bankruptcy in 2010.[2]

It's well known that setting a business plan is a critical means of achieving change, helping transform a concept of what the future should be into reality. However, many organizations fail to see that developing a blueprint for rapid change also serves as a vital tool for motivating employees to go above and beyond their current reach.

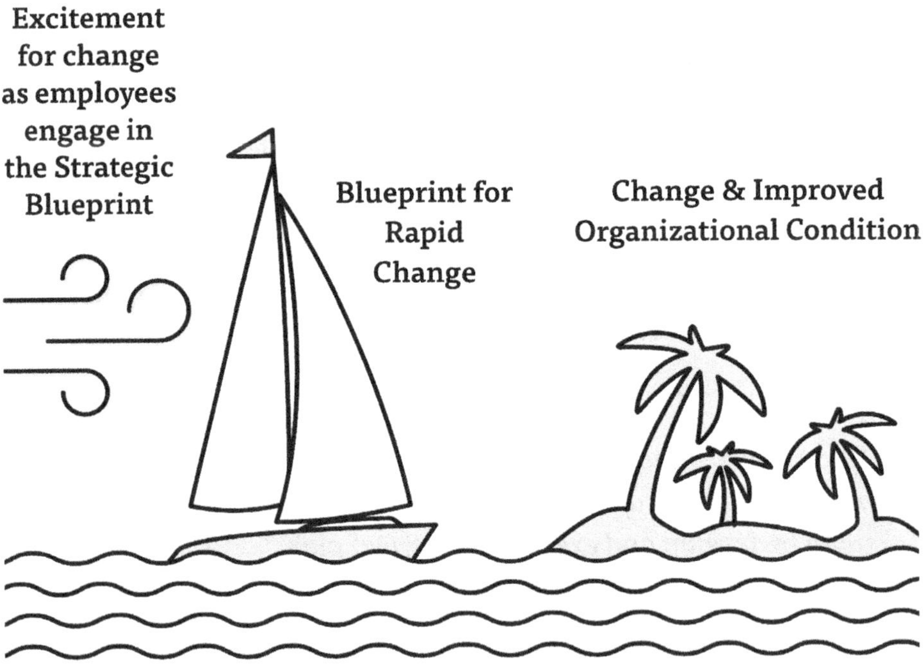

A division of PricewaterhouseCoopers recently conducted a survey of over 540 people from a wide spectrum of industries and backgrounds. They found that high-impact strategic planning efforts hold immense potential to inspire employees.[3]

The Swedish furniture giant IKEA, whose mission statement is "to create a better everyday life for many people," employs continuous goal-setting as a tool to motivate its employees and continue their growth. The facts speak for themselves. By the end of FY2023, IKEA expected to continue its pace of opening stores in 50 new locations and 17 new markets each year.[4]

If nothing else, setting the game plan for the future is a healthy exercise in that it provides multiple benefits. It helps shape tomorrow's outlook for the company and the atmosphere in which it will operate. It also assigns accountability for the prescribed outcomes that are delineated. At the same time, it forms the basis of the rewards that will be awarded to the team that helps bring those strategic objectives to fruition.

Pharmaceutical company Merck's asserted purpose is to use the power of leading-edge science to save and improve lives around the world. Another example of a robust strategy is that of the US Air Force: "The World's Greatest Air Force—Powered by Airmen, Fueled by Innovation."

Both strategic directives include commitments to principles that will serve as a means to bridge the gap between the real-world issue they're in business to address and the required solution. Each one is also evergreen, in that the higher calling of saving lives or being the world's greatest Air Force and maintaining those audacious yet noble objectives may never truly be achievable. These goals can only be met and maintained through long campaigns that last for generations. In effect, each corporate blueprint serves as a trumpet blast to herald and rally the troops that are part of the organization to contribute to a purpose greater than the organization through commitment to a set of principles that require character and steadfastness.

Setting a roadmap also provides the operation with a means of comparing some future reality against the backdrop of what that future state should look like, given the strategic objectives that were set. This provides senior leadership an evaluation tool, which, in turn, allows them to determine if the establishment is missing the mark, and if so, by how much, as well as what needs to be done to right the ship.

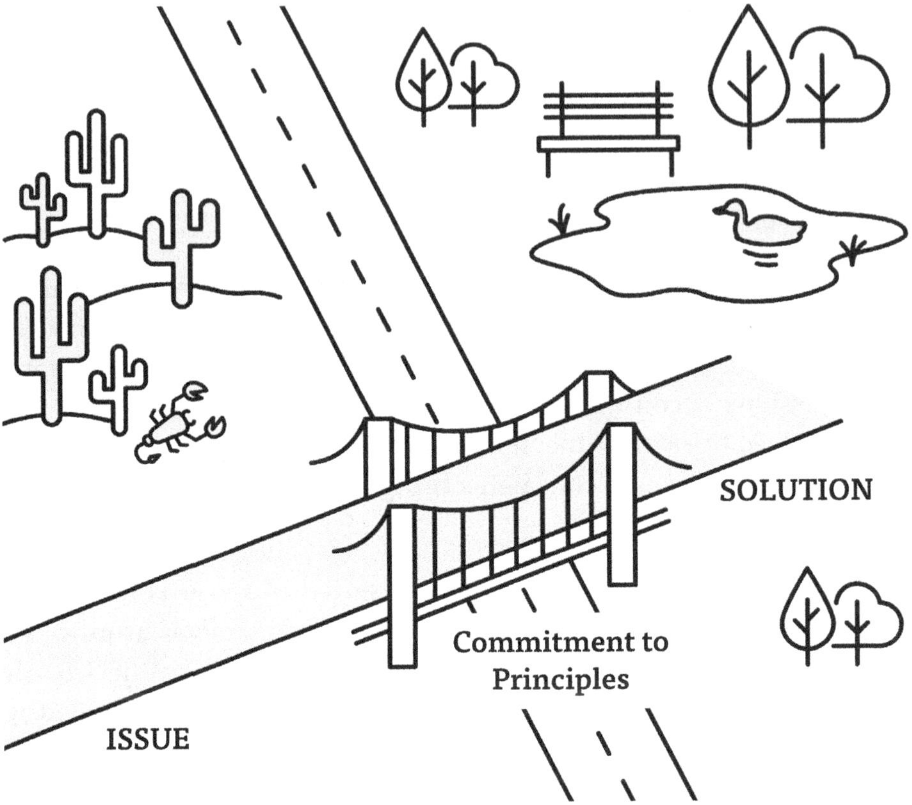

Thus, in this way, having a documented set of strategic objectives for senior leadership to appraise their performance serves the same function an annual performance appraisal does for staff employees. It allows the team to assess what they've been able to complete, and to determine what can be done to bridge the gap between what was planned versus what was accomplished.

However, for all of these positive benefits, the most compelling reason to develop corporate strategy (and to revisit it on at least an annual basis) is because the strategy-setting process itself can be an extremely motivating tool. As a matter of fact, in my personal experience as a mid-level manager, nothing breathed new life into the doldrums of everyday organizational life as being included in strategic development. The very act of sitting in a room with senior leaders and my counterparts from every major organizational discipline to chart out the future of the firm was nothing short of exciting. It afforded me an opportunity to forge my own destiny and take much needed respite from those dreary concerns that I was completely dependent on senior leadership to set all goals, expectations, and job responsibilities.

> *However, for all of these positive benefits, the most compelling reason to develop corporate strategy (and to revisit it on at least an annual basis) is because the strategy-setting process itself can be an extremely motivating tool.*

It also allowed me insight beyond the horizon of what I was able to discern as a project manager and mid-level manager in the trenches of organizational life.

Like any tool, however, it must be wielded correctly, and the rules of the game have drastically shifted.

Strategizing the Strategy

After spending years in business planning, I learned there are several facets that need to be considered before action strategy development can be successful. Before scheduling a strategy session, carefully consider the following.

While what I am about to cover might seem onerous, consider the cost of assembling a team of the highest-paid professionals in your enterprise and taking them away from the daily fires they're expected to put out. What a waste of time and resources it would be if you discovered that the planning roadmap will fail from the start because it was not appropriately set up to succeed.

Be Flexible and Intentional

The tangible outcomes that are expected to come from planning sessions should be identified. This goes well beyond such basic factors as time horizons and which efforts should be expanded vs. what new market segments to consider entering. The group needs to also tackle the most pressing dogmatic issues, risks, and concerns the organization is facing in light of the larger economy in which it exists. For example, specific questions—such as how to gain increased investors to fund future real estate ventures in a high-inflation, high-interest-rate environment—need to be considered. In addition, consider broader, open-ended facets, such as the cultural, internal, and external landscapes in which the venture finds itself operating.

It's not what is said, it's who says it that counts.

Not only does game plan formulation need to happen via open and honest discussion, with feedback being solicited from everyone in the room, but it also needs to include the right players. This also goes beyond the basics of including senior leaders from operations, finance, marketing, technology, and the like. This means that senior leaders need to determine a means to get line management and line level employees involved as well.

It Takes Money to Make Money

Without meaning to restate the obvious, strategy takes time and money. Not surprisingly, a budget needs to be created and the appropriate amount of funds set aside in order to fund those strategic objectives that require additional funds. I've witnessed robust, well-planned strategies fail simply because daily operations out-prioritized strategic efforts, since strategy execution efforts were not allocated hours and funding.

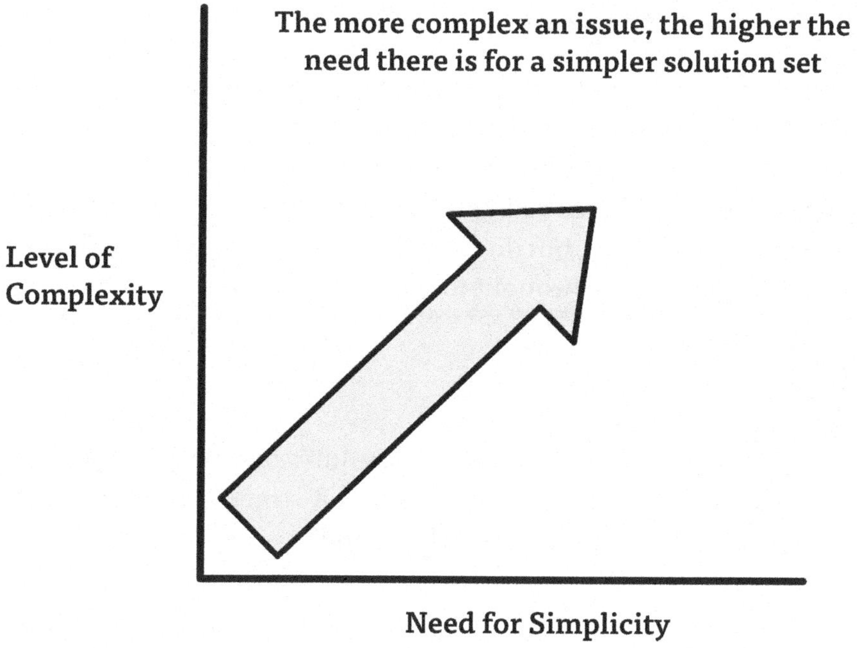

Map out a high-level framework of how the strategy will be met.

It's not enough to construct an execution plan to ensure strategy is achieved. The implementation plan needs to be both robust and flexible to allow for all unforeseen circumstances that will inevitably create delays to plans that are too rigid.

A recent study uncovered the fact that anywhere between 60-90% of all strategic plans never even get initiated. While the reasons vary widely, execution was the main culprit, time and again.[5]

It's imperative that the enforcement plan is written in a manner and expectation that allows for pivots in its execution. In fact, the enforcement of business planning itself needs to be reviewed on a consistent basis to ensure it can be continuously tailored to dynamics of the internal and external environments.

Setting static, unexamined, and sterile application of planning objectives guarantees change efforts will border more on the unattainable and idealistic than what is applicable and necessary.

Aim High or Miss the Mark

It's beyond critical that senior leaders commit to and sponsor the strategic plan. To do otherwise would lead only to frustration, fatigue, and distrust among the workforce. However, senior leaders must not get in the way either. Make it a point to set the plan and get out of the way of those that roll it out, but do make certain to be present whenever issues and bottlenecks are brought to your attention.

I experienced first-hand the absolute train wreck that takes place when senior leaders strong-arm a strategy, only to revert to a peripatetic engagement at best, and to essentially disappear shortly afterwards.

We had worked assiduously alongside senior leaders to construct a strategy for a multibillion-dollar effort that would completely re-organize the way over 5,000 personnel completed operations, finance, collective bargaining agreements, and HR functions from coast to coast. Once the strategy was set, senior leaders delegated the implementation of business initiatives to department heads of the equivalent rank and authority. What ensued was infighting between geographically separated units, resulting in a year-long stalemate at best, and many ruined work relationships at worst.

We completed execution of our change initiative, but had to forge agreements along the way that dampened the value the outfit would have realized if the strategy had been implemented as it had initially been established.

Team Work Does Not (Necessarily) Make the Dream Work

None of the benefits that strategy development provides can be fully realized without the use of a team. However, that team must be dedicated, empowered, and organized in a manner that takes every cardinal objective and treats it as an autonomous, albeit interrelated, project.

Questions to Consider

- *Are your strategic objectives implemented in a systemic and organized manner? Or, is implementation scattered across a sea of existing priorities that never really see the light of day?*
- *Do you solicit and include the input of line-level employees who are in the trenches of day-to-day organizational life when developing strategy? Why not?*

CHAPTER TWO

WITHOUT VELOCITY, STRATEGY IS DEAD

Today, we operate in a business landscape that makes it seem as if we stand on a precipice in the midst of a maelstrom—a knife's edge where dozens of small and large adjustments need to be made with tremendous terminal velocity just to live another day. Despite the milieu of the business environment in which we have been thrust, the majority of firms take three times longer to develop and execute strategic initiatives than they can afford to wait.[6]

A study conducted in 2010 made the disheartening discovery that Americans spend almost half of their waking hours merely thinking rather than focusing on the work that's right in front of them.[7] This means that approximately 165 million people relegate an average of eight hours a day to ruminating on their problems, discomforts, goals, possibilities, and scores of other thoughts rather than taking action.

Amazon serves as the perfect illustration of how rapid execution is pivotal. With the demise of former retail juggernauts JC Penney and Sears, the Internet retail company is snapping up these once bustling stores in an opportunistic thrust to slash delivery times.[8] As a result, as early as 2019, Amazon was giving FedEx Ground a run for its money when it undercut its contract with them for holiday deliveries—simply because Amazon's delivery channels could deliver its packages quicker than FedEx itself![9]

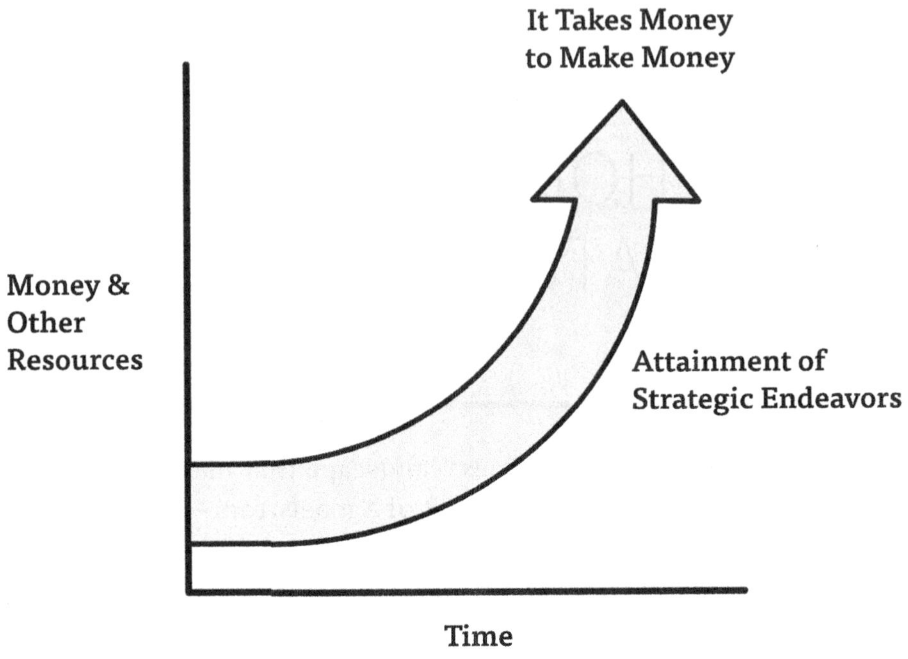

Without delving into the plethora of homilies about the importance of enjoying the present and not investing too much care about the future, Its paramount to consider the fact that all we have as people, parents, investors, or business executives are the moments that are right in front of us. That's all the canvas on which we truly get to paint the future we envision.

While the countervailing point that it also makes sense to devote some time to simply thinking is true, executives behind the wheel of an entire organization simply do not have that luxury.

Your Competition Is Outpacing You

In today's fast-paced world, companies are making time-to-market and quick pursuance of planning efforts a competitive advantage. In fact, a study launched by McKinsey & Company revealed that companies whose core capabilities centered around the speed of strategic implementation benefited from a 30% jump in financial performance.[10]

This is a great statistic if you happen to be one of the few companies that focuses on time to implementation, but the reality is most businesses struggle to plan for what's coming next year, let alone planning to shorten implementation. This sobering reality points to the need for senior executives to make it a practice to develop strategic plans, but also the need to implement with intense and focused velocity.

In fact, a study launched by McKinsey & Company revealed that companies whose core capabilities centered around the speed of strategic implementation benefited from a 30% jump in financial performance.

The cost of *not* prioritizing implementation is market share lost to competitors who can simply implement faster. The best and brightest plans and objectives are meaningless without swift action to make them a reality.

Airbnb started out by renting out three air mattresses and is now one of the most burgeoning tech companies around. In the process, they've virtually changed the way people travel. However, things were pretty grim at the beginning, when the founders saw that their rental rates were dismal. They even resorted to selling cereal to make ends meet! But they turned the company around when they improved listings by making them more aesthetically pleasing and attention-getting. Within a month, sales doubled, then tripled, and the rest is history. Airbnb went on to revolutionize the travel industry (without having to sell cereal for a vocation).

One of the primary leitmotifs of the Air Force is to "fail fast and fail often." While this phrase is not exclusive to the Air Force, the point that organizations need to pull all the stops and take risks is not lost. The driving principle behind this emphasis is our enemies are relentless in increasing their warfighting capabilities, so we must be the same.

In the race for market share, the velocity by which strategic planning is executed is paramount.

This is also true for Corporate America. Our competitors are constantly seeking new ways of gaining market share, increasing margins, reorganizing, and utilizing technology in order to dominate their industry. There is no time for corporate leaders to plan out the perfect implementation approach.

In the race for market share, the velocity by which strategic planning is executed is paramount.

Problems Get Worse with Time

Business leaders are barraged with an onslaught of issues ranging from turnover and declining profits to personnel issues—and a whole host of other burgeoning quandaries that never cease.

These issues are commonplace, but they turn catastrophic when allowed to remain in place without any action taken to resolve them.

Common issues such as declining market share only get worse as the competitive and economic landscapes shift around us. Left untreated (or undiagnosed, which is even more egregious), loss of market share only gets worse unless swift action is taken. Any problem—known or unknown—will continue to plague the organization with increasing destructiveness unless swift action is taken.

In the home entertainment industry, Circuit City had 567 stores and 34,000 employees at the time it was forced to liquidate. The company failed to innovate rapidly in order to put a stop to Best Buy's rapid growth and encroachment on its market share. Circuit City became reactionary versus visionary, while its competitor, Best Buy, made revolutionary adjustments, such as directly linking products from nascent tech startups to its network of existing customers.

A study conducted in the UK a few years ago found that of the 1,900 companies examined that became insolvent, more than 72% of them averted taking any action against the problems that ultimately led to their demise.[11] That's the equivalent of playing a game of chicken against an oncoming semitruck while driving a hundred miles per hour!

The key issue is senior leaders feel they need to craft the perfect campaign against the real problems the enterprise is facing, when the reality is completely different. William of Occam, a medieval monk, asserted that the simplest solution to any problem is the best solution. In the same manner, Occam's razor is true of the business landscape in which we operate.

When faced with a multimillion issue we discovered on a new radar system for a United States Space Force (USSF) client, our practice assembled the finest and most sophisticated minds known to man in the world of radar.

At the end of several weeks (and over $2M in salaries and program delays), the solution to the issue was not found in intricate statistical and modeling analysis, or in new designs to the radar itself, or even in a more powerful radar. The answer was found simply by talking to future users of the system who identified a few very simple workarounds that would allow the radar to work in the real world—even if it did not meet the most exacting technical requirements.

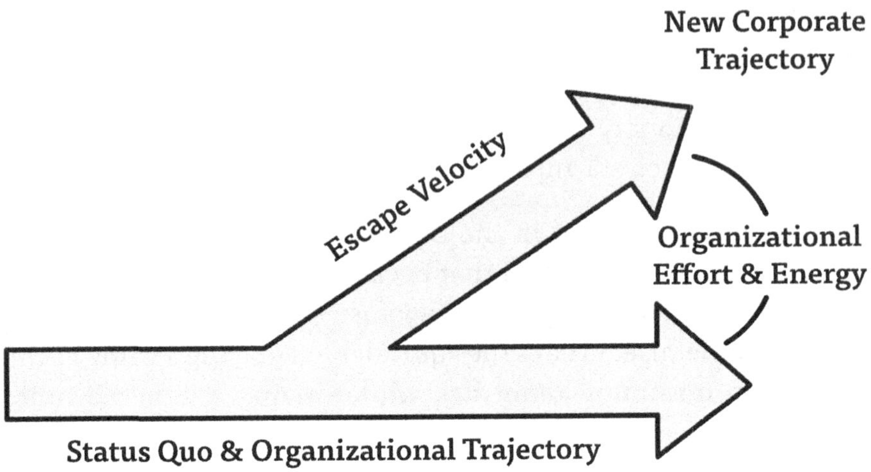

Organizational Attention Deficit Disorder

Great plans and objectives quickly lose momentum if they aren't immediately acted upon after their genesis. Not only does the passion behind strategic planning dissipate with increasing acceleration with every passing day, but the organization responsible for carrying this out also gets saddled down by the daily grind. As soon as the team vacates the lofty halls of the boardroom, war room, or whatever appellation the group designates for the gathering location, they're off checking the dozens of emails and actions, presentations, calls, and conferences for which they're responsible. It's not surprising that within a few short days of the planning sessions, everyone present during planning has either completely forgotten or is wholeheartedly trying to shirk the actions they were assigned.

It's no wonder why, in a recent study cited by the *Harvard Business Review*, 60 to 90% of all strategic plans never make it out of the boardroom.[12]

This scenario is infinitely exacerbated when the "death spiral of planning" takes hold of the organization. Invariably, as companies approach implementation in an enervated fashion, all the shine and appeal of planning objectives lose their luster and the planning roadmap gets relegated to mere lip service in boardroom status discussions and staff meetings. A few months—or even years—later, the problems plaguing the company become insurmountable, and a new series of strategic planning meetings is launched. Because implementation efforts are languid and lacking once again, the cycle repeats itself. After a few rotations of this death spiral, employees appropriately assign new strategic plans with a flavor-of-the-month epithet. This in turn cements the probability any strategic plans that are promulgated and thrust through the boardroom will be dead on arrival.

Rather than allow a changing landscape to erode market share, companies like Chipotle reacted quickly to the COVID-19 pandemic by hiring 10,000 employees and adding drive-through lanes to multiple locations. These "Chipotlanes" were added to over a hundred stores in order to accommodate customers concerned walking into the store could risk coming into contact with someone that had the communicable virus.[13]

One of the first major strategic initiatives I was asked to help lead was the third attempt to overhaul an organization. The first effort, affecting a population of 5,000 that spanned the East and West Coasts, failed soon after planning sessions with top-brass military officials had ended. The second attempt died after line organizations resisted the initiatives and senior leadership left for other endeavors. Finally, 12 years after the first attempt at bringing about strategic change, my team was brought in to develop new initiatives and implement the change that was so drastically needed.

The key lesson I learned was that implementation could not be delayed. Every week's delay caused a stagnation that took two weeks to break through.

Time Is Money

The longer it takes to implement planning, the more money bleeds out of the organization.

Every day that reduced market share, profitability, or high turnover buffets and plagues the company's performance is another day the organization bleeds money. It's not surprising to find that, based on a study of over 6,000 executives, vacillating execution of the strategic roadmap is the #1 consternation for CEOs and the top risk CFOs desperately try to mitigate.[14]

The opposite notion also holds true. Organizations that can pull the trigger on strategy execution with an unwavering focus on maintaining the terminal velocity required to break through the status quo reap the benefits of a 77% leap in profits.[15]

Quite simply, there is no time to waste when it comes to executing the action plan, since the costs of not turning the ship around are staggering at many varied and multidimensional levels.

Success Is Only Attained Through Failure

The overarching philosophy of Corporate America regarding the purpose of companies' existence is that the firm exists to succeed. Perhaps the clearest example that has been seen by most, and cemented this philosophy in the culture of American companies, hails from NASA's almost militant "Failure is not an option" incantation that helped launch America's nascent space program of the 1950s.

However, the countervailing view—that unless companies fail, they cannot achieve success—is neither a proverb nor a concept to be thrown away. The merits of this principle are observed time and again throughout history. In his book, *Make Change Work for You*, Scott Steinberg discovered that 90% of companies change their strategic direction in order to experience growth.[16]

The ever-popular toy known for decades now as Play-Doh® was initially created in the 1930s as a household cleaner that could remove coal from wallpaper, but the company learned through trial and error that its product was better at entertaining kids than cleaning wallpaper!

I've been witness to the mission success that was achieved whenever one of our US Space Force clients adopted the switch in philosophy that transitioned from being risk-free to becoming risk-adopting. Instead of holding on to a "failure is not an option" perspective, they adopted a "fail fast, fail often" approach and reaped the benefits of a twofold increase in operating capability across several suborganizations.

Perfection Kills Profits

One of the main drivers of the malaise that plagues implementation is the panic senior leaders often undergo at the thought of launching the organization into implementation without a rallying, well-architected strategy. All too often, executives fall prey to the notion that they must devise the perfect long-term plan, and at once they begin to contemplate every potential adversity, risk, and failed outcome that might remotely be possible. This internecine effort hampers management's ability to attain the vision of tomorrow and employees' capability to implement the strategic roadmap given to them, since the expectations are unattainable.

In his quest for perfection, *Moby Dick*'s Captain Ahab became so entranced by the notion of bringing his elusive and arcane enemy to annihilation that he brought about his own untimely death. In the same manner, the pursuit of perfection quickly becomes an anchor that instead of propelling us to the farthest edges of performance clamps us down and entraps us in the bog and mire of false expectation.

Seeking perfection is a costly endeavor at best. Delays in new product launches alone can cost 15–35% of potential returns.[17]

Unless it's coupled with swift application, strategic planning becomes nothing more than a means of formally creating false expectations, emaciating the faith that line-level employees have in senior management and opening the door for competitors to gain headway.

Questions to Consider

- *How effective are your strategic efforts in terms of time to implementation?*
- *Do you consider your firm's ability to implement strategic change quickly a core capability? If not, why not?*
- *What would it mean for you to have the capacity to implement strategic planning in a quick, effective, and structured manner? Increased market share? More revenue? Less turnover?*

CHAPTER THREE

THE PERILS OF PLAYING IT SAFE

It was heralded for weeks leading up to the showdown as the most epic game in 20 years of college football. The fateful 1966 match between the #1-ranked Notre Dame and undefeated Michigan State left fans on both sides of the stands bewildered and disillusioned. The Fighting Irish entered the stadium in that fabled game in a lofty position: They could claim the top spot with either a win or a tie.

Both Notre Dame and Michigan State fans entered the stands with the expectation that their teams would fight to the bitter end in order to edge the other team out—regardless of the lofty position Notre Dame held coming into the game. After all, this was exactly what the fans had come to expect. Each team had fought tooth-and-nail to have a shot at competing against the other.

Michigan State managed to surge to a heroic comeback from a 10–0 deficit, tying the game. Notre Dame fans were confident their team had the fight, bravado, and wherewithal to break the 10–10 stalemate and secure the win. After all, isn't that what #1-ranked teams do to maintain that lead?

As the game clock dwindled down to the two-minute mark, with the Fighting Irish in possession of the ball, storied Notre Dame coach Ara Parseghian elected to give up the fight and simply played for the tie. While this act of omission still paved the way toward a national championship, fans' disappointment hit a crescendo they had not had to endure until those last two fateful moments. This timid move dismantled the character of what was just moments before the paragon of the competitive spirit of college football.

Notre Dame and Michigan tried their best to avoid even the slightest potential of making a mistake. The result was they ran out the clock, finishing with an unimpressive tie.

Rather than go on the offensive and plow through uncharted waters fraught with danger, leadership teams shrink back into the placid waters near the shoreline where nothing is likely to be lost, nor can victory be seen.

What those fans had to endure is similar to what must often be tolerated in boardrooms, hallways, cubicles, and back offices of an astonishing myriad of businesses worldwide.

Rather than go on the offensive and plow through uncharted waters fraught with danger, leadership teams shrink back into the placid waters near the shoreline where nothing is likely to be lost, nor can victory be seen.

That won't work for technology firms. IBM has committed to invest a monumental $100 billion over the next two decades, against the backdrop of intense competition from Chinese tech companies, to ensure it maintains its competitive position.[18]

Similarly, Micron, one of the foremost leaders in semiconductors in the US, recently announced that it will invest up to $100 billion over the next two decades to create a plant in New York.[19] The goal is to help the US tech industry gain an advantage against global competitors.

Another storied semiconductor firm, Wolfspeed, has announced it will invest in semiconductor production in North Carolina.[20] This is part of the joint campaign by leading semiconductor firms to maintain their stalwart advantage in the industry, despite the seemingly carte blanche pocketbooks of competitors who are encroaching on their market share at break-neck speed. Directly engaging with competition makes absolute sense when market dominance, and, in fact, survival hangs in the balance.

To put it in the words of our 26th president, Theodore Roosevelt, "Far better is to dare mighty things, even though checkered by failure, than to rank with those poor spirits who neither enjoy nor suffer much, because they live in a gray twilight that knows not victory nor defeat."[21]

At the same time (and perhaps not surprisingly), risk-reduction programs abound in every corner of industry. In my former role as project manager for complex technology programs, I would spend hours on end defining the risks that were likely to plague the project and simultaneously create mitigation plans to shield the project from those risks as much as possible.

Managing risk is prudent and helps create a culture of economy and discernment, but it should be done while also taking the offense to gain undiscovered market share, increase the company footprint on a new product line, or spearhead efforts to gain entrance on a competitor's stronghold.

Over 65% of all businesses fail ten years after being formed.[22] Corporate leaders have no other recourse than to learn how to take offensive measures, take on risks, and learn to become comfortable being uncomfortable. It's literally a matter of life or death!

Occupational Hazards of Playing It Safe

There are a host of dangers associated with failing to take first blood and striking out into the unexplored. On one end, our contenders do their research on what we do and how we do it for the sole purpose of being able to predict what we're likely to do in the future. This provides our corporate adversaries an absolute advantage and the high ground when it comes to the battlefield over market share.

In fact, a *Harvard Business Review* article asserts that the ability to predict competition and how competitors will react to your actions is a must-have when it comes to long-term planning.[23] The easiest way to establish a pattern that our competitors can use against us is by playing it safe, since that simply requires we maintain the status quo.This issue is found in almost all firms across industries. In a study conducted by the *Harvard Business Review* across more than a thousand employees, less than a third asserted that their company executives made any semblance of an effort at changing the status quo—ever.[24]

Refusing to step out and tread uncharted territory means you cannot reach a better, more lucrative end state. Conversely, it also means you will leave well-entrenched tracks behind for the competition to sniff out your location a mile away.

Executives seem to believe the only way to step into the ring and out of the status quo is by taking large leaps into the unknown, such as Toyota's $400 million investment in flying car technology. The reality could not be farther from the truth. Small, steady improvements in process improvements invariably lead to dramatic leaps in business value. The key is not to think of charting a different course akin to jumping off a cliff with a faulty parachute, but rather one more in line with taking different routes along your daily walk in the park.

Coca-Cola was deemed to be in the Top 50 Most Innovative Companies in 2021 rankings not because it took a quantum leap of faith into the fourth dimension but simply because it reduced its brand list by half to streamline operations and increase efficiency.[25]

Reaching Out to Avoid Crossfire

One of the more significant leadership lessons I learned while in the military was the need to keep team members "gainfully employed."

That meant I had to provide people with work that was challenging and dynamic. The difficult-to-achieve goal of yesterday had to be replaced with a different goal today. Otherwise, boredom quickly set in, like bacteria that can infect even the healthiest and energetic of team members. The effects of boredom bacteria, when left untreated, led to broken windows, absenteeism, entering the wrong apartment after a night out of drinking, and DUI incidents.

While this may be more typical of a military outfit with newly minted high school and college graduates than it is of your typical rank-and-file business employee, the point that boredom leads to conflict still holds.

The *Harvard Business Review* studied the ill effects of workplace boredom and found that almost two-thirds of all employees in the US are bored, detached, disillusioned, or a combination of all three.[26]

We have all seen the typical symptoms of boredom among team members and the conflicts, wasted energy, and the traipse-and-wander that follows. At this point, even menial tasks can take diving-catch efforts from middle management to get everyday tasks accomplished.

In stark contrast to most firms and their bored and disillusioned staff, Adobe employees express their excitement about working for a company that regularly solicits its line members for solutions to meet the changing needs of its customers and its workforce.[27]

Perhaps it's also not surprising that the company has a chief people officer among its officer ranks to ensure leadership can keep a pulse on staff sentiment.

Playing it safe does not provide shelter from the storm—it plants the seeds of mutiny instead.

Looks Are Deceiving

In my role as a project manager, it was often my job to decide what to do with risk. The majority of the time, I would devise a mitigation plan to take control over those things I could, and that would generally lead to results like avoiding technical issues or simply keeping stakeholders happy.

However, there were other times when I decided to do nothing at all. Commonly known as the "do nothing" approach for you risk managers, this would seem like the right thing to do, especially when things were out of my lane and I had no tangible method to make an impact. Unfortunately, the scenarios would invariably go from bad to worse as the days and weeks flew by. There's some kind of law in play that causes untreated risks to worsen with time.

At one point, I decided the software issue we encountered in a test flight was most likely a simple fix that would not affect any other part of the avionics system. While that might have been true, if we had decided to pull the thread further, we would have discovered a much more systemic problem with the software code that would result in thousands of pounds worth of bombs missing their target by a mile or so. The only saving grace to this event is that the bombs were dropped on a test range and not a target surrounded by civilians!

While gaming juggernaut GameStop enjoyed precipitous growth from 2005 to 2015, due in large part to the pop of real estate values in the wake of the Great Recession, it has been in steady decline for the last several years.[28]

Perhaps one of the most blatant mistakes the gaming retailer made was not mitigating the risk of the development and growth in digital, virtual gaming. This would mean its customers would have no need to physically purchase gaming equipment at any of its 4,000+ stores. Why would you drive to the neighborhood GameStop when you could log on at home and begin playing immediately? Why risk a wasted trip, only to find out the game you had been eagerly anticipating was out of stock?

This trend in digital gaming has been quietly surging for years as game and gaming console developers migrated to an all-digital solution. It's therefore not surprising that CDs and other physical media are now just antiques purchased for nostalgia and relegated to antediluvian forms of storing games. Unfortunately, GameStop did not react to this trend and is now reporting a loss of sales in the hundreds of millions. At the same time, the cost of owning real estate across their more than 4,000 stores has taken its toll in the maelstrom of increased inflation and higher interest rates.

What looks good on paper can result in catastrophe. Avoiding confrontation might seem prudent, but it ultimately lays the foundation for failure.

Working for a Living

We need to forget the flawed perception that executives are there to lead the firm through placid waters, where everyone riding the ship can be sheltered from stormy seas. On the contrary, executives are paid the big bucks to be at the helm. They intentionally pilot the ship through murky and uncharted waters in that somewhat perilous journey so that it might drop anchor at shorelines where greener pastures await.

Not only is risk-taking a paramount skill for executives to master, but research also shows that employees' respect for leadership skyrockets when they display their willingness to take on the unexplored.

For years, the most respected engineering minds placed a limit on the ability of a manned aircraft to fly faster than the speed of sound. The adeptly named sound barrier would cause all aircraft designs created from the early 1900s through the mid-1940s to evade even attempting supersonic flight.

However, the US Air Force set a course to prove whether or not that speed barrier could be broken. On October 14, 1947, just months after the Air Force gained its independence from the Army, Colonel Chuck Yeager took Glamorous Glennis just past the elusive sound barrier, causing the first-ever sonic boom that could be heard across the Mojave Desert. This daring act literally heralded the jet age with a bang. Recounting what special blend of skills this test pilot must have had, in his heralded book Tom Wolfe aptly called it "the Right Stuff."[29]

In my opinion, all that the "Right Stuff" boils down to is grit and a willingness to take on risk—two factors I strongly believe most senior leaders can readily employ.

Harley-Davidson was on the brink of bankruptcy in 1981 because its market share had been emaciated down to a meager 15%. Competition from Japanese motorcycle companies had all but run the company out of business. It was then that Richard Teerlink took the helm and led the company on a journey with the goal of attaining increased quality, improving customer service, and delivering world-class heavyweight motorcycles. The results are history; this fabled icon of a company now captures a greater-than-50% market share, almost $2 billion a year in sales, and tattoos of its name are found across a staggering amount of males of riding age.[30]

Organizations, like all other living organisms, do not do well without exposure to those elements that can simultaneously cause harm and growth.

All living organisms known to man require light and hospitable conditions to develop, grow, and sustain life. The only exception to this rule is, of course, fungi, which are entirely happy living in a sequestered, damp, dark, and lifeless environment.

Organizations, like all other living organisms, do not do well without exposure to those elements that can simultaneously cause harm and growth.

Questions to Consider

- *Are you playing it safe? Or, are you consistently taking those risks whose rewards have the potential to catapult your company across new thresholds?*
- *In what endeavors would you engage if you knew you could not lose?*
- *How might your employees' perception of the organization shift if they knew they were part of a risk-laden adventure that required all hands on deck to succeed?*
- *What would it mean to you to help navigate those uncharted waters and untraveled terrain?*

CHAPTER FOUR

FORGET THE NORMAL LINEUP

We now do business in a world that has vastly departed from once conventional practices that will never again see the light of day.

> *The team you need to assemble to tackle the issues revolving around the new not-normal landscape of today cannot be made up of the team of yesterday.*

Instead, we are in what I call a new and permanent "not-normal." This "not-normal" consists of multiple pivot points that range from new, more stringent health restrictions, where two-thirds of employers around the world have completely restructured work to allow some of their employees to work from home. This is just one change that's here to stay, including the acceleration of digital transformation, forcing organizations to consider technology as a strategic and core competence, rather than a byproduct of tech refresh.

The team you need to assemble to tackle the issues revolving around the new not-normal landscape of today cannot be made up of the team of yesterday. Mixing old approaches to accelerate business in today's arena will lead to disaster. The countervailing is also true. We have to learn to let go of what worked in the past in order to pursue endeavors better suited for success in a new and shifting set of marketplace conditions.

Yasuo Takeuchi, CEO of the Olympus Corporation, took risk in selling the company's profitable microscope business, upon which the business had been built, to focus on new lines of medical technology products. In the same vein, Takeuchi braved selling Olympus's camera business in 2021 after deciding that the shift in its customer preference for smartphones instead of standalone cameras meant the company had to shed one of its stalwart product lines.

When asked why he was making such drastic changes while at the helm of a firm steeped in tradition, his reply hit the nail right on the head: "We had to move before it became too late."[31]

Your Team Is Not Equipped to Tackle Strategy and Change

Traditional functions and departments such as operations, finance, and marketing are not prepared to deal with the level of rapid strategy development and implementation that's now a required core competency of the business. The rate, depth, and scope of change are beyond the grasp of yesterday's means of organization.

Today's environment calls for a different approach to strategy. Who develops and executes business planning also needs to be as varied as the pivots, speed traps, and bends in the road in the macro environment in which the organization operates.

Peloton enjoyed a rapid increase in revenue during 2020 and 2021, when the pandemic and the ensuing stay-at-home restrictions meant that people shifted their means of exercising from local gyms to at-home fitness equipment. However, the lifting of restrictions that began in late 2021 and 2022 shifted preferences back to working out at gyms, which allowed people to use a range of fitness equipment at a fraction of the cost of a Peloton product. This pivot cost Peloton $2.8 billion in revenue in 2022 and a 94% drop in its stock value.[32] While the company is working at a feverish pace to do things differently, such as overhauling its sales model and production processes, only time will tell if these moves will have come too late in the shift in customer demand to make a difference.

Recent research into the rate and effectiveness of change in which firms engage reveals that two-thirds of businesses must restructure their organization four times every five years.[33] Unfortunately, and perhaps not surprisingly, these reorganizations are met with abysmal results, since only three out of every ten of these initiatives are deemed successful. What's worse is that the rate of change in play today will only gain velocity. Companies will have to be prepared to pivot on a dime, anticipating changes that have not yet materialized.

In a study published by the *Harvard Business Review*, it's shown that a significant reason why change efforts are associated with such an atrocious success rate is senior leaders continue to use levers with which they're comfortable, instead of those who are commensurate for the change that needs to be made. Different scenarios require different approaches, tools, teams, and organizational structures to combat the risks associated with changes in scenarios.

Senior leaders must conduct a bottom-up restructuring of the organization's hierarchy, communication, business planning, and change management processes. In addition, this restructuring efforts needs to be taken on with a sense of urgency if today's firms are to thrive over the next five, ten, and thirty years down the road in a landscape of supply chain issues, geopolitical upheaval, technological revolution, and an aging Baby Boomer population that will take with it decades' worth of tacit knowledge and experience as they retire.[34]

Businesses worldwide are on the edge of a precipice that can only be bridged by positioning themselves to take on and bend the dynamism of the current landscape to their advantage.

Work Harder, Not Smarter

Executives need to do the heavy lifting of acquiring the talent and organizational structure needed to bring about rapid and meaningful change. To start, senior leaders must hire experts at change management, transformation, and technology adoption to ensure the business is agile. They must also recruit strategic planning and implementation experts, such as project management teams, to lead the change effort with the level of commitment, professionalism, and organizational structure typically required of long lasting, value-laden change.

Enphase Energy, a California-based manufacturer of home-based solar and storage products, employs a diverse team of strategic planning experts located across diverse global markets and locations in which its customers reside. Their job is to continuously identify and evaluate a diverse set of opportunities that the company can exploit. This approach is tied to the company's foundation of employing metric-based, continuous improvement to constantly position itself in the most advantageous stance. The goal is not merely to react to changes in the market, but rather to anticipate, plan, and act upon potential shifts that are a few years out from materializing.

The results of this approach to business planning speak for themselves, as Enphase stock reported fourth-quarter 2022 adjusted earnings of $1.51 per share, representing a 106.8% leap from the $0.73 cents reported in the prior-year quarter. In addition, the Enphase bottom line flew above and beyond Zacks Consensus Estimate of $1.27 by 18.9%.[35]

Don't Get Left Behind

It's extremely easy to lose sight of the firm's future talent pool and succession plans, but ignoring this widespread, albeit insidious, issue comes at a huge cost. Skill shortages and high turnover rates among younger workers only exacerbate the problem further.

Yet, research shows that bringing on a younger workforce helps foster innovative insights and approaches that often provide solutions to historical issues plaguing the organization.

> *It's extremely easy to lose sight of the firm's future talent pool and succession plans, but ignoring this widespread, albeit insidious, issue comes at a huge cost.*

A 2020 Harris Poll showed that 30% of the workforce will be comprised of Gen Z workers by 2030.[36] Senior leaders have ample opportunity to profit from this emerging opportunity by taking the initiative to hire younger employees. Bringing in employees who have freshly arrived on their career path will also strengthen business planning and execution efforts, particularly as the company tries to forecast and plan for emerging trends that are still a few years out.

Research recently published by *HR Director* found that Millennials and Gen Z employees are forecast to help rake in over $1.5 trillion in additional profits by 2045, since they represent the engines of the knowledge economy.[37]

However, in order to keep this talent pool over the long haul, executives need to ensure the organization is ready to provide the culture that Millennials and Gen Z workers embrace. Prioritizing work-life balance, providing agency, establishing open lines of communication, and adjusting pay and incentive systems to mirror this younger culture are paramount to preventing turnover with a generation of employees that value life outside of work and are being valued perhaps more than by any other generation we have witnessed.

The conventional model of who formulates strategic planning in today's dynamic economy is akin to using an abacus to solve a complex math problem. The tool itself may have a vintage charm, but it's largely useless unless used as a paperweight. Senior leaders need to place the right teams in the driver's seat and become comfortable being the race director, orchestrating chaos into a symphony.

Questions to Consider

- *Are your planning efforts beating the market? Or, are you constantly playing catch-up to the ever-changing business climate?*
- *How far out is the horizon for your strategic planning efforts?*
- *What would it mean if you could plan for and exploit the forecasted changes in the business environment two to three years out?*
- *Are you involving the* **right** *people in the planning process? Do you have a stagnant and unflinching roster of traditional functional areas that form the typical lineup of who develops plans and forecasts? Or, are you active in delegating planning to those in the organization who have their finger on the pulse of the market?*

CHAPTER FIVE

TRADITIONAL STRATEGY IS SEVERELY CONSTRAINED

While the world has been made smaller through technological advances and new means of communication, it's also expanded the business planning horizon to colossal new heights. However, over 90% of firms today are woefully myopic and robotic when it comes to the strategic levers they pull to reach their desired destiny.

In the words of Mark Twain, "It ain't what you don't know that gets you into trouble. It's what you know for sure that just ain't so."[38] A recent study conducted by McKinsey noted that over 90% of all profit and loss centers are statistically tied to last year's budget.[39] In other words, less than 10% of organizations have leaders at the helm that are willing to try bold new initiatives and the budgets tied to them, and leave last year's planning efforts where they belong—in the past. Instead, senior leaders avoid the opportunities that are constantly presenting themselves and elect to keep their planning efforts small—completely swerving away from big, bold moves. This behavior results in nudging the needle just above the final resting place where it's settled for years. The company might manage to eke out a few meager points of margin or an unimpressive increase in market share, which inflation renders useless.

Top-flight executives make it a habit to steer clear of the insidiously lethal comfort zone. Jon Siegler, co-founder of the software firm LogicGate, concedes that while the risk of failure increases with the launch of each new product or service, the potential payoff is much, much higher.[40]

It's What Helps That Hurts

The everyday rut, disguised as "expertise," keeps capable organizations in the dark doldrums of lackluster performance and stagnating growth. Constantly chasing after last year's plans can quickly transform into psychological handcuffs that tie companies to out-of-date paradigms and strategies that simply cannot flex to the hyperdynamic market changes of today. Business planning sessions need to begin by planning for what has not been planned. Business leaders need to forecast for upcoming trends that might impact customer demographics, alternative uses, and customers for existing product/service lines, and posturing for flexibility when unexpected opportunities present themselves.

The everyday rut, disguised as "expertise," keeps capable organizations in the dark doldrums of lackluster performance and stagnating growth.

Lyndon Hanson, George Boedbecker Jr., and Scott Seamans created a comfortable, slip-on, clog-like shoe made from flexible and slip-resistant resin (named Croslite) over two decades ago.[41] While they thought the clog-like footwear contraption was ugly, they also knew it was comfortable and would be perfectly at home for people with a boating pastime. Not surprisingly, the first pair of Crocs debuted at a boating show in Fort Lauderdale in 2004. What is surprising is that what was considered an ugly yet functional boating shoe became a product that brought in $2.3 billion in sales in 2022, has been transformed into platforms and heels, is worn by high-fashion aficionados, and is now sold at 7-Elevens across the US, starting at the end of 2022.

The Fast and the Spurious

The adage that things in life are often not what they seem is more real and impactful to the bottom-line than ever. The pace and extent of change today far outpaces what it was yesterday, and that tempo will only increase with time.

The ascent of the smartphone dismantled the market for flip phones and myriad other related tech products. While certain industries were somewhat shielded from these disruptions in the past, the latest round of technology leaps will cast a far wider net and catch almost all industries by surprise. AI, machine learning, cloud-based data storage, deep-fake technology, and the security vulnerabilities these skyrocketing capabilities have introduced is enough to leave even the most sophisticated CTO crying uncle. The only certainty is that businesses must anticipate, plan, and take action in adopting or responding to these industry upheavals. Failing to plan for this wave of change will destroy the bottom line, leaving these companies in the dust and behind those that are adeptly leveraging these increased capabilities.

The pace and extent of change today far outpaces what it was yesterday, and that tempo will only increase with time.

Retail AI, the use of automation, data, and technologies to deliver highly personalized shopping experiences to customers, is already being used by tech-savvy companies to determine demand twelve months or more into the future, move inventory quickly, and price products in a manner that takes into account what the business climate will be a year or more out.

Sandeep Unni, senior director and analyst for Gartner, asserted that he has seen artificial intelligence integrated across a spectrum of retail functions and inlaid to become part of routine business processes and daily operations.[42]

Defense giant Lockheed Martin and software colossus IBM recently announced a partnership aimed at providing the Department of Defense (DoD) the capability of revolutionizing AI processing. The DoD is so confident it can leverage this technological upheaval that it has amplified its investment in AI from $600 million in 2016 to well over $2.5 billion in 2021.[43]

This tech transformation will allow small, tactical military platforms, such as drones, to process colossal amounts of data within minutes so they can provide the warfighter the battlefield advantage in an emerging tech-driven world where every inch must be hard-won.

Just like the field marshal of old—or the fleet admiral of today—today's business executive must stay ahead of the tidal waves of change about to hit the shoreline by broadening business planning horizons by a factor of ten—or risk the ability to live and fight another day. For all the risks they represent, the frantic tempo of business change and leaps in technology have also created a landscape that is chock-full of opportunities for savvy business leaders on the lookout for them.

Stop Playing Follow the Leader

The notion of competition and its application are grossly uninformed in today's business culture. The idea that the only means for companies to survive is through directly competing against, well, the competition is misinterpreted and exaggerated. This myth can be found in every nook and cranny in the field of business strategy, when it only actually applies in a few applications where the effort itself is architected around the notion of directly competing against your opponent, such as football, chess, and arm wrestling.

Aside from these somewhat fun yet rarely occurring events, in the world of business, direct competition need to be reserved for very specific circumstances that seldom take place.

Executives would do well to ignore the competition altogether and wholeheartedly invest in those efforts that are propelling the company to new heights. This is much more effective than sniffing the trail for where the competition is heading in the hopes that the company can take second or third place at best—or ending up in the same unfortunate and desolate destination in which the competition has been languishing.

Executives would do well to ignore the competition altogether and wholeheartedly invest in those efforts that are propelling the company to new heights.

Steve Jobs ignored competitors while he was laboring away at bringing the transformative concept of the iPhone to market. All the while, the competition was fervently striving to make incremental product advancements in the world of flip phones and eke out a few small increases in market share percentage.

Despite growing consumer concerns over inflation and a seemingly imminent economic downturn—all amid the backdrop of a strong dollar—former Walgreens CEO Roz Brewer made strides to grow the business in ways that were head-and-shoulders above its competitors. Walgreens recently invested over $5.2 billion to acquire VillageMD and transform itself from a conventional drugstore chain into a full-fledged health care company. While investing that much money amidst economic turmoil is certainly a risky move, Walgreens estimates the payoff in this investment to be $12 billion by fiscal year 2025.[44]

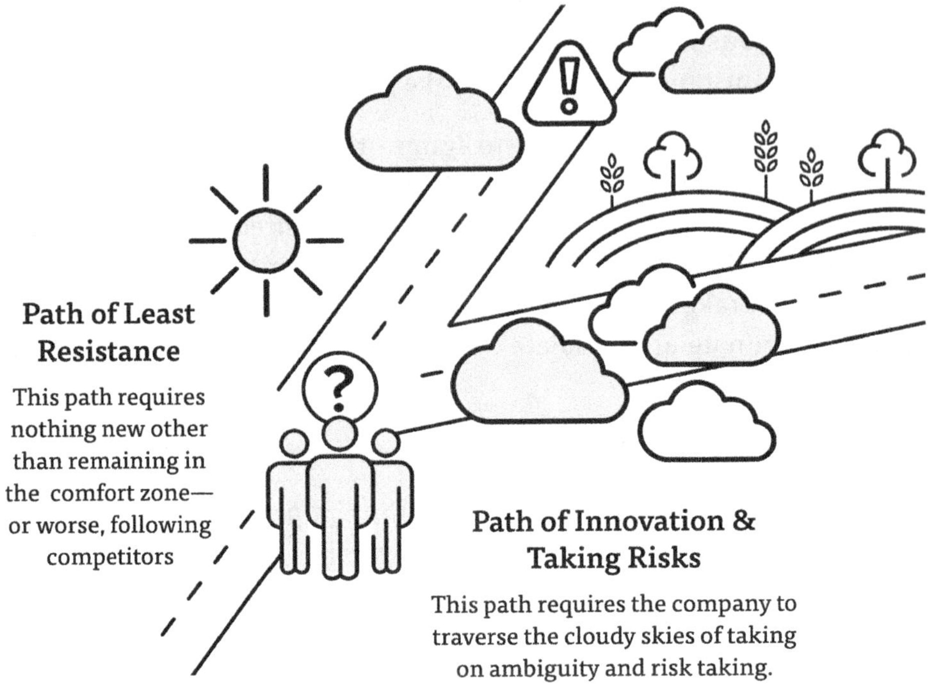

Business leaders need to start painting the future with their own canvas instead of retracing the often lackluster portraits of rivals.

(Traditional) Teamwork Does Not Make the Dream Work

There are times and places to strategize with internal corporate colleagues, but drastic times call for drastic measures. Going at it alone and taking on the horde of risks and upheavals by yourself does not make a hero out of a company. What it really does is leave it isolated, defenseless, and clueless.

In recent years, the US Air Force has realized that its only option is to partner with industry on its highly sensitive mission of maintaining air superiority for the US, its allies, and interests if its capabilities are going to stay relevant with the pace of technological change. This point was emphasized at an exchange between Air Force and industry leadership at the Mission Support industry day held recently in the city of San Antonio, TX. The purpose of this exchange was to capitalize and leverage private-sector ideas in order to bridge any gaps in capability of which the Air Force might not even by aware. In fact, the Air Force has set aside over $4 billion to partner with industry and transform Tyndall Air Force Base (AFB) into a power projection of the twenty-first century.[45]

In the same manner, companies need to strike partnerships with suppliers, vendors, companies that engage in industries similar to but different from their own, suppliers, vendors, and even "competimates" (direct competitors that are trustworthy partners on at least a temporary or project-specific endeavor).

The purpose of these atypical partnerships is simple: leverage insights, capabilities, and networks in order to reach a market niche that is unattainable, and generally turn risks into opportunities. While the concept is straightforward, making it work in practice can be difficult to navigate. However, the focus should be on agreeing to specific outcomes, with accompanying metrics that will reveal if the strategy is on-plan or off-track.

Sheri Schmelzer partnered with the founders of Crocs after realizing the flower she threaded on her family's many pairs of Crocs would be just as well-liked by the public. Soon after she discovered this, she and her husband started Jibbitz to start selling her Croc accessories nationwide. It turns out she was right on multiple levels. Crocs founder Lynden Hanson saw the advantage he could leverage by tapping into Sheri's market share, and he ended up buying Jibbitz just a year or so after its inception for $10 million, with another $10 million on the table if Jibbitz could meet profit projections.[46]

Risks Are to Be Exploited, Not Avoided

I've yet to see an organization's demise come as the result of taking too many risks. On the contrary, in most of the organizations with whom we have worked, the death toll came as the result of the insidious perception that avoiding risks will lead to profit and growth.

The business planning process needs to carve out a minimum of 10% of the budget for high risk/high pay-off initiatives. This needs to be further partitioned out into projects that will:

- Exploit new market segments.
- Require new products or services.
- Require new talent to accomplish.
- Lead to a 10:1 payoff between tangible and intangible value.

One of the best ways to get on the inside track with these higher-risk initiatives is to strike temporary partnerships with organizations that have similar strategic interests but different capabilities and market segments that your firm—and theirs—can leverage. Even if these partnerships are temporary, senior leaders need to have the ability to forge partnerships that will help the company take on ventures it would not otherwise be able to make and to spread the risk of the journey across organizational boundaries.

mCloud Technologies Corp, a cloud technology firm that provides performance optimization of energy-intensive assets, recently asserted that it is partnering with Google Cloud as part of its go-to-market plan to deliver its AssetCare sustainability solutions to customers worldwide, leveraging Google Cloud infrastructure.

This means customers using mCloud's AssetCare service will be able to onboard and integrate more quickly, reducing deployment time and allowing mCloud to deliver value to its customers in a condensed timeframe.

mCloud forecasts this partnership will also yield a 25% improvement to its cost structure as both companies provide the funds necessary to take on this go-to-market effort. The ability to share the burden of sales & marketing and research & development will also provide mCloud with cost benefits over the long term, well past initial product launch.[47]

Partnering can yield substantial value across tangible and intangible spectrums, including increased networks, capabilities, market reach, reduced costs, and, ultimately, corporate growth that would not be attainable otherwise.

Perfection Will Lead You Astray

The reason many of us don't try new approaches to strategy comes from fear of failure.

As business leaders, we often strive for perfection because we think that's what's required of us. We need to hit the mark and set a new benchmark every time. The reality that this perception is unhealthy, unproductive, and exhausting is in large part what creates high turnover. In fact, studies show a correlation between socially induced perfectionism—such as that prescribed by a boss—and burnout, depression, and other mental issues. These deleterious effects can spell catastrophe for even the best-positioned companies.

Senior executives, by nature of their office, are the leaders to whom the organization looks and are therefore in the best position to demonstrate a healthy relationship between wanting to reach lofty goals and being okay with less-than-perfect timing and results. If we're not failing, we're simply not trying hard enough to grow our organization.

Questions to Consider

- *Do you tend to steer the company away from endeavors that are uncomfortable? Or, do you see those as opportunities or challenges that will serve as a catalyst for growth? How does your planning budget reflect these perceptions?*
- *When was the last time your company partnered with another firm?*
- *Are you and your employees comfortable with failing fast and often while endeavoring for high-risk, high-payoff ventures? Or, do you avoid high-risk opportunities like the plague?*
- *What challenges and risks have been taken to place the company in the position of advantage it enjoys today?*
- *How might that same drive change the business in the future, and what would that mean to you? Higher pay? Taking that vacation you've dreamed of? Buying that dream house? More time off? Early retirement? Happier employees and less turnover? A better night's sleep?*

CHAPTER SIX

ANTIQUATED METHODS, MEDIOCRE RESULTS

Unlearn What You Already Know

To sum up the preceding chapters on business planning in as concise a leitmotif as possible, organizational leaders must not only commit to continuous learning, but must also ardently work to turn that into a core competency.

Executives need to be passionately driven to seek new experiences, take on new challenges, and harness this penchant for lifelong learning to spark the same drive in the hearts and minds of employees.

In a study published by the *Harvard Business Review* about those factors that lead to success in our post-COVID business world, the resounding chime of success is only struck for those that are lifelong learners. In fact, continuous learning is now considered an economic imperative for companies that are serious about long-term growth.[48]

Executives need to be passionately driven to seek new experiences, take on new challenges, and harness this penchant for lifelong learning to spark the same drive in the hearts and minds of employees.

Toyota executives turned the disaster of the 2011 Tohoku earthquake and ensuing tsunami into a learning event that was leveraged during the COVID-19 pandemic. This led the company to cruise by competitors, like GM, and become the 2021 top automotive seller of North America.

Through their relentless drive for continuous learning, top executives turned the 2011 natural disaster into a learning opportunity and were able to identify those parts in its supply chain that are most vulnerable during macro-level disruptions. As a result, Toyota stockpiled enough supplies to carry them through the worldwide disruption caused by the pandemic. They also used the 2011 event to sharpen their pencil on lead times. In doing so, they perfected their inventory planning while simultaneously enhancing their approach to suppliers and supplier relations.[49]

What You Know Keeps You Old

While it's true that formal education can serve as a platform from which a career can be built, it can also cement boundaries that can never be moved to accommodate exponential growth.

I've been in organizations where learning new approaches to accomplishing the organization's core business was not emphasized. The unwavering result is boredom, restlessness, and lackluster motivation from employees at all levels. And, of course, year-end performance failed to meet the mark, leaving senior leaders to come up with remedies that would inevitably simply treat the symptom, not the disease.

A company that lacks the drive to learn constantly and explore leaves its employees bereft of the excitement, vitality, and purpose that learning provides. It's not surprising that employees caught in the doldrums of stale and complicit companies become disheartened, disinterested, frustrated, and dissenting in their daily slog in the trenches of corporate life. This is akin to the inevitable boredom that wells up within those kids that are quick learners, have mastered the material, and are now wearied by the slow pace of the classroom. The only recourse is to immerse these students in a fresh and continuous stream of new opportunities and challenges. In the same way, lifelong learning keeps rank-and-file staff alive and equips them with a fresh renewal of energy, commitment, and continuous innovation that will vault performance, year in and year out.

Nearly 71–90% of companies that participated in a post-COVID study regarding the impact of upskilling employees to gain a broader range of proficiencies asserted that the initiative resulted in greater fulfillment of strategic plans and bolstered employee performance and satisfaction, as well as raising the company's brand among staff and customers alike.[50]

Axonics, a global medical tech firm that cranks out novel products aimed at treating bladder and bowel dysfunctions, reported a staggering 25,401% leap in revenue from 2018 to 2021, with a total revenue stream of $180.3 million at year end FY21. When asked what led to this seminal jump in revenue, CEO Raymond W. Cohen asserted that part of the right mix was the company-wide pledge to continuously innovate. Not surprisingly, Axonics was also included in the Deloitte Technology Fast 500 (a ranking of the 500 fastest-growing tech, media, and telecom, among several other industries) companies for the second year in a row![51]

From a cultural perspective, continuous learning helps bring about equality among the rank-and-file. When encouraged across the firm, access to new concepts and improved ways of doing business acts as an equalizing force that helps place employees at varying levels and roles in equal standing.

Ray Mabus is the board chair of InStride, which specializes in working with organizations to provide tailored training curriculum to its employees. He asserts, "If we're going to be competitive as companies or states or as a nation, we have to reach the people who are already in the workplace."[52]

Not only does continuous learning motivate employees to develop, but it also leads to career growth, increased employment opportunities, and a more equitable landscape across the entire labor market. Ryan Roslansky, CEO of LinkedIn, believes that in this economy distrust between employers and employees can be severely heightened.[53] In these turbulent times, it has become critical for hiring managers to focus more on specific skill sets so they can place people at the right time and place for the job. Consequently, hiring managers should focus less on "antiquated signals" like a college degree and a similar pedigree, which is now becoming increasingly inaccessible to the average person.

Let Go and Let Live

Times of fast-paced change require renewed commitment to learning new perspectives to stay ahead of upcoming changes. Just like it's good practice to remove old, unused furniture from one's house, organizations need to let go of old perspectives that are either no longer true or no longer serving their firms' needs for continued prosperity and growth.

Business planning should not only consider tangible initiatives that should be undertaken but should also explore what portions of the company's perspectives need to be revamped, why they need to be revamped, what new perspectives need to be developed, and how they will be pushed across the enterprise. Perspectives help build corporate culture, which in turn will steer the company to a tragic conclusion or to the lofty end intended.

For several years now, tech companies in particular have been trying to stay ahead of the pace of change that riddles business planning, in part by shifting their perspectives across leadership, innovation, cultural, and technology facets.

HMG Strategy, the owner of a digital platform that arms tech executives with the ability to reimagine their enterprise and the business world, announced that it shattered sales records in 2022. The company attributes this leap in revenue to increased demand for its global advisory services and its sponsored events as its clients see the need for shifting perspectives to keep pace with the consequences of our volatile macroeconomic climate.[54]

> *Business planning should not only consider tangible initiatives that should be undertaken but should also explore what portions of the company's perspectives need to be revamped, why they need to be revamped, what new perspectives need to be developed, and how they will be pushed across the enterprise.*

Needless to say, shifting perspectives can come with huge payoffs. Prime Pinnacle, a leading venture capital firm, discovered that it paid to back a shift in perspectives about food delivery from traditional brick-and-mortar to lunch trucks. In recent years, the lunch truck business model has exploded across multiple venues, including education, as schools across the country were looking for ways to combat an 85% rejection rate of school lunches.[55]

Faster and Funnier

While the value of learning new concepts and approaches is tantamount, it's not enough. If the learning process is going to run idly by in the background—devoid of a sense of purpose, timeliness, and without clear objectives tied to metrics—that activity will not get the company anywhere. How else will you know if the learning is tethered to business value?

That scholarship must be done quickly and deployed almost immediately thereafter on an ongoing basis so that it can be grounded in real-life application before the theory evaporates on the work floor.

In the words of James Caufield, strategic specialist at the digital manufacturing company Protolabs, "Whoever is moving the fastest is going to define what the future is, so really it's those people who are going to decide what the next big advancements are. You can only be there first if you're the fastest."[56] This is in relation to the news that several firms in the modern space industry are experiencing rocket explosions shortly after launch—and are happy to write that off as a learning event from which they can benefit.

In the words of James Caufield, strategic specialist at the digital manufacturing company Protolabs, "Whoever is moving the fastest is going to define what the future is, so really it's those people who are going to decide what the next big advancements are. You can only be there first if you're the fastest."

Ford Motor Company's smallest division, Electrical and Fuel Handling, packs a powerful profitability punch, despite its size and tough competitors. Although the division lacks the resources of larger groups at Ford, it has emphasized the criticality of organizational learning in order to reach new heights among its workforce of 7,000 with average annual sales of $1.5 billion. Dubbed the Ford 2000 program, division leaders instituted this multitiered learning change effort of rapid, organization-wide learning in order to countervail increasing world-wide competitiveness, reduce costs, and significantly grow its current customer base from the US to foreign shores.[57]

The results of the Ford 2000 rapid learning program demonstrate its efficacy beautifully. Earnings have leaped dramatically, product launch costs, time-to-market, and capability have increased every year, quality metrics have skyrocketed by double-digits, and the division has saved millions of dollars of warranty costs. As if this was not enough, the division has also managed to cut 50% of product launch budgets across its product portfolio, and it now leads all Ford divisions in its achievement of Total Productive Maintenance Checkpoints.

Old Dog(s), New Tricks

People often make the flawed assumption that the only way an organization can learn is by taking on all of the effort independently. In reality, one of the most effective methods of ingesting new skills is by partnering with those companies who are already practicing those proficiencies, albeit in a slightly different market, product, or service. This could include combining two seemingly disparate capabilities and combining them to create a completely new product or service. Leveraging the skills of another company to create synergy and embark on an endeavor that will create significant benefits should be constantly considered as part of the learning strategy of the firm.

One recent example of such a partnership involves CODA Automotive and Mullen Automotive. Founded in 2009, CODA Automotive started life as a fledgling electric vehicle (EV) automaker, joining the dozens of other nascent EV car makers of that decade who wanted to make a run for the potential windfall revenues available in the early days of the alternative energy automotive market. Unfortunately, like many of the other smaller auto manufacturers of their day that did not strike gold in the EV gold rush, CODA found itself filing for bankruptcy in the 2014 timeframe.

It was at this time that Mullen Automotive acquired CODA, under the stewardship of David Michery. David was both an investor and veteran in the entertainment business and a life-long car aficionado. David had launched several efforts to manufacture electric vehicles that could be sold within a price range affordable to the target customer and would return the profit he desired—all at once.

After realizing he could integrate all he had learned about EV manufacturing with the expertise CODA had racked up in developing EV battery systems (something Michery had not mastered), the dream of being able to develop an EV of his own design was reborn and the Mullen Five concept was also brought to life.

Forecast to be available in 2024, the Mullen Five will have a range of approximately 325 miles, a 155 mph maximum speed, and a lightning-fast 0-to-60 jolt in only 3.5 seconds, with an impressive battery-pack life of 95 kilowatt hours. All this is thanks to CODA's expertise in EV battery systems and Michery's love of EV vehicles.[58]

While this particular example involved an acquisition, there are myriad similar opportunities that can be achieved by simpler and less involved partnerships. These can bring new platforms, markets, and paths that lead to unparalleled growth, renewed excitement, and transformation—for each party.

Do Not Stay the Course!

The only consistent facet of business life we have now and for the foreseeable future is that of constant change. This stream of new developments and disruptions requires new approaches to provide the firm an opportunity to forecast upcoming forks in the road, at best, and possibly guide the nimble pivoting necessary to stay on that road to growth and success.

While this business environment can be alarming, to say the least, these risks are also masked opportunities and a treasure trove that should be exploited.

In fact, about half of all Fortune 500 businesses were launched during times of economic, political, and/or social crises, underscoring the notion that times of upheaval, for all the discomfort they dish out, can also provide promising conditions of growth for those companies that move with that perspective.

Fortune magazine noted that such household names as FedEx, Hewlett Packard, Microsoft, and LinkedIn were once fledgling, nascent underdogs that were incubated during times of world war, depressions, recessions, runaway inflation, and deflation. The list can go on and on, but you get my point.

Now is the time to make investments in new approaches, partnerships, and new lines of business with a stance of flexibility and agility to take on this dynamic course. Let's take these times for what they are: a small but promising opening in the fabric of the business cycle that allows us to jump in and help steer the company, whether embryonic or industry veteran, and lose sight of the seashore with full steam ahead.

Questions to Consider

- *Do you feel excitement about the current and forecasted business climate as an opportunity to venture into the unknown? Or, does a knot in your stomach develop as you wince at the obstacles thrown in your direction?*
- *When was the last time you embarked on a new initiative as a direct result of forecasting what you thought was going to be a shift in the market, customer demographic, or your own labor force? How well did it go? What approaches could potentially have been considered that might have had a positive impact on that outcome?*
- *How engaged are you in ensuring your staff is enthusiastic about the current circumstances and the future?*
- *Do company leaders and employees take on new perspectives and challenges on a consistent basis? Or, is there angst any time a new initiative is embarked upon?*
- *Are you taking intentional steps toward identifying new opportunities, partnerships, and learning engagements that would launch you into new areas of growth and profitability?*

CHAPTER SEVEN

DON'T WALK THE TALK—TALK & CHALK THE WALK

Put Down the Playbook and Pick Up a Paint Brush

Earlier in the book, we noted that a manager's real job is to push down decision-making autonomy to the most qualified employees. In that sense, a manager is more like a coach leading the football team across the field to a victory than the archetypical senior executive who sits behind the desk and dictates all the strategic twists and turns the company makes.

Once senior leaders have architected the framework that addresses what is needed for victory and the bench is stocked with the right players at the right time, the real job of senior management begins: using broad strokes to paint the picture of where the company should steer toward and what it should become in the process. Senior leaders need to do this on a continual basis, since the painting itself is a living, evolving mural requiring different colors, accents, and changes to keep the end game in view as the environment around and within the company shifts.

While it's the employees who are closest to obstacles that are in a great position to map out the most efficient means of getting beyond those hurdles, it's the senior executives that must constantly communicate what the end game of the strategic rollout will mean to the entire company. More importantly, they must articulate what arriving at that destination will look like for the average company employee. Senior managers must provide inspiration to the rank-and-file across the broad spectrum of the organization that the destination is worth the journey. In the eloquent words of a mentor of mine who has been part of major corporate shifts as a sales manager for Caterpillar, "Management must determine if the 'the juice is worth the squeeze.'"

> *Once senior leaders have architected the framework that addresses what is needed for victory and the bench is stocked with the right players at the right time, the real job of senior management begins: using broad strokes to paint the picture of where the company should steer toward and what it should become in the process.*

The burgeoning sports e-commerce retailer, Fanatics, elucidates the need for CEOs and senior leaders to be artists when it comes to painting the compelling canvas of what the company needs to become in the future with an enthusiasm that is contagious to the rank-and-file. This bombastic organization has exploded in growth in the short span of a few years, reaching a recent valuation of $27 billion. They've attracted a windfall of investors, including the NFL with a $320 million investment. But as with all companies driven by an exciting and audacious vision, Fanatics admits that it's nowhere near the ballpark in which it wants to play. The company's goal is to transform into a $100 billion juggernaut over the next decade.[59]

It's no surprise that Fanatics' CEO Doug Mack has been successful in his ability to draw an exciting vision of the future. In fact, the company was recently included in *Insider's Top 25 Large Companies* list of companies whose employees were deemed to have the best CEOs at the helm of the ship.[60] When speaking as to what makes Doug Mack a fantastic senior leader, they unanimously clamored that he is exceedingly "visionary and transparent as to the direction of the company." They added that Mack's "messaging through town halls is lively and engaging."[61]

This ability to paint a lively picture of what the future holds—should everyone steer toward the same outcome—has set the company ablaze. As long as Mack's ability to paint the fresco of tomorrow continues, it will be no surprise to watch Fanatics reach that $100 billion valuation in a decade—or perhaps even sooner.

Don't Count the *How* Before You've Considered the *What*

Not only must corporate leaders paint a picture of what the future looks like, but they must also be dogged in their pursuit of elucidating what the organization needs to be in that future state. While a handful of leaders are adept at depicting a vision of the future in terms of goals and metrics with vivid paint strokes, even the best of these paint a picture that is vacuous with respect to exactly what the company needs to become. This painted canvas of the future—with its parochial emphasis on lag metrics such as gaining 10% market share in untapped markets—insidiously leads the rank-and-file to assume that meeting lofty goals metrics are all that really matter—all other things be damned.

Executives must absolutely couple their depiction of the future vision in terms of goals with a clear rendering of what exactly the company needs to become in this pursuit. Leaders must forge what tomorrow should look like with an unwavering commitment to form the organization into what it needs to become in terms of identity, culture, and ethos in its journey to that future state. This requires that leaders carefully consider where the company is in terms of its development, take inventory of its current set of values, and include in their painting of the future what values need to be ingrained deeper into the company ethos and which values are yet to be adopted.

Companies with a strong identity also have a deep sense of mission and values from which all other major endeavors derive. Trader Joe's, one of my personal favorite places to shop, is one of Southern California's hot spots for out-of-the-norm tasty foods offered in a relaxed atmosphere. With over 500 stores, Trader Joe's abides by a few key values: "wowing" its customers, *kaizen* (i.e., "change for the better"), integrity, and being product-driven.[62]

The team at Salesforce.com, over 60,000 strong, rallies under the banner of "bring companies and customers together." The company adopted a series of core values that led to its success and to being consistently ranked among the top places to work. Its core values revolve around the focal points of trust (acting as trusted advisors), customer success (they consider themselves successful when their customers succeed), and equality (everyone across the company deserves equal opportunities).[63]

And, of course, this brief set of examples would not be complete without the mention of a company with an exemplary and strong corporate identity. With over 10,000 employees, boasting perhaps one of the most recognized brands in recent history, Nike's challenge to all of its customers to "Just Do It" has helped propel this juggernaut to the loftiest of heights. But behind the background is where the foundations for Nike's success have been laid. Their four core values of innovation, team inclusion and empowerment, making positive social and community impacts, and following sustainable business innovation have served as their cornerstones.[64]

For all of the success stories revolving around having a strong identity, there are many other companies that are guilty of failing to determine who they were—particularly as the environment around them was in a dynamic state of upheaval—and they paid the price for it. Further, while some organizations that were once household names invested in brand identity at their outset, they did not quite redefine what their identify could become in terms of delivery of their product or service, in light of industry shifts, and in response to competitors' moves.

In its heyday, Blockbuster Video was a blockbuster of a company, providing customers a perfect means of entertainment for a weekend or evening at home. Unfortunately, when movies began to be made available via streaming, Blockbuster did not shift its means of providing entertainment to its customers and filed for bankruptcy in 2010, marking the end of an era.[65]

Mean What You Say

There's a tendency among senior managers to mix their message with platitudes, niceties, and an overt tone of levity that can downplay the complexity of the vision of the future. While the senior leader must paint a picture of the future in a manner that draws inspiration from the entire workforce, he or she must also include the potential potholes, detours, cliffs, and valleys that will be encountered in what is painted. That panorama must include what the team will likely need to become in order to arrive at their destiny, without which the sojourning team will end up shipwrecked, hijacked, or starved along the route.

> *While the senior leader must paint a picture of the future in a manner that draws inspiration from the entire workforce, he or she must also include the potential potholes, detours, cliffs, and valleys that will be encountered in what is painted.*

Yes, the language used must be colorful and vivid and emphasize why this journey must take place, but you must also talk about what's ugly, what will be uncomfortable, and what gaps need to be bridged. The messaging that goes along with strategy setting must be meaningful, not simply because the journey's end is important but also because you mean it and you are emotionally and financially sold on the idea and how it's communicated. The message that's used to covey the essence of the future must be lean and mean, without any superfluous language.

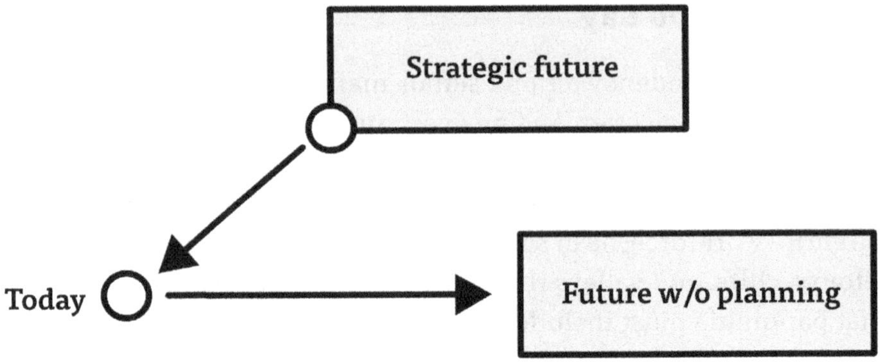

Executives need to paint what the strategic future should look like & work backwards to identify when and what skill sets need to be achieved and identify what roadblocks will likely be encountered

When having to face the tough consequences of economic slowdown coupled with stagnating productivity amongst the rank-and-file, Google CEO Sundar Pichai had to make his message clear and concise: "It's clear we are facing a challenging macro environment with more uncertainty ahead." He added, "There are real concerns that our productivity as a whole is not where it needs to be for the head count we have."[66] This simple but painfully true message adroitly addressed the heart of the issue the company was facing in a manner that did not resort to finger-pointing or calling out certain divisions by name. Instead, Pichai chose to address the entire organization about the critical need for increased productivity amid deteriorating performance.

While directing the ship at Google, Pichai did not dictate how the problem was to be solved. He only highlighted the need for change that had to happen for Google to become what was envisioned at the outset: a company that, as asserted in its 2004 Founder's IPO letter, is "committed to significantly improving the lives of as many people as possible."[67] Pichai got to work by soliciting the help of all 170,000 of Google's employees in combatting the company's efficiency issues rather than dictating a solution set he and his close circle of executives could have created on their own.

Strike the Right Chord at the Right Time and the Right Place

To continue with the Google example, the message about where the company needs to go to become what it needs to be must be concise. A verbose, convoluted message with even a couple of superfluous twists and turns will derail and dilute what you, as the leader, are trying to get across. Hence, Pichai's message was to the point, and he laid out where the company needed to pivot, when, and how in about 50 words.

Beyond ensuring that messaging is concise, we must be sure to use the right words to strike the right chord among employees. Just like playing an instrument, the message needs to use words in such a way that the message is harmonious to the audience. The words you choose must be imbued with a tone of empathy, insight, and a strong call to action. However needed and timely a message might be, if it's delivered in an unharmonious manner it will sound like the jarring scratch of chalk on a blackboard we all remember from elementary school. The effect will be more that of a wrecking ball than a surgical instrument of precision.

To further illustrate this, Google's CEO's plea to solicit the help of company employees illustrated the point that he's not capable of turning the ship around without the help of those closest to the problem. This vulnerability created that sense of empathy, insight, and a call to action that is vital to striking the right chord and creating a harmonious message.

Finally, not only must you deliver the message in a crisp and harmonious manner, but you must also deliver it at the right time and place, otherwise it will be drowned out by the noise of everyday corporate life. Playing a quartet in the middle of a busy intersection during the evening commute on the hottest summer day of the season would not likely have the soothing, relaxing effects produced if it were played in a fully acoustically modified symphonic hall, replete with an atmosphere of amity and calm. In the same vein, messages of strategic weight have to be delivered in the right venue, one where the delivery of the message will fall on attentive, focused, and anticipating ears.

While there is no hard-and-fast rule as to what the venue should be, there are clear examples of what it should *not* be: email, company instant messenger, the quarterly corporate newsletter, relayed back to the rank-and-file by middle management, etc. The message must be delivered in a venue that allows the entire corporate family to receive it at the same time and in the same way—from the second in command to the newly hired summer intern.

In an effort to ensure the entire company moves toward the same message, Proctor & Gamble uses an approach they call the P&G Connect Plus Develop program. This crosspollination approach commissions multiple teams within and outside the company to marshal everyone toward the same objectives, all while simultaneously soliciting feedback from multiple disciplines. This ensures that the change is not only well-communicated but also refined and implemented in a holistic technique as well.

P&G's efforts have been effective. Way back in 2000, only 15% of the company's innovation efforts met profit and revenue targets. Fast-forward to late 2022, when Jon Muller, P&G CEO, asserted, "Every innovation we have delivered in the market has created value, and continues to create value and contribute to our results."[68]

Questions to Consider

- *Do you use colorful, vivid language to deliver strategic messages clearly and enthusiastically, company-wide? If all employees were to be asked to name the top three strategic initiatives for your company, what percentage of them would be able to answer correctly?*
- *What would it mean if a majority of the company's employees was excited and hopeful about the direction the company is taking?*
- *How do you message matters of strategic weight to the rank-and-file? Is the message delivered at the right place and time and with empathetic tones and optimism? Or, is it robotic, mundane, and routine? Does it elicit compelling emotion and drive to charge forward and drive positive change? Why or why not?*
- *How much effort do you put into assuring company strategic initiatives are created and implemented in a holistic, multi-disciplinary manner? When was the last time you commissioned outside help to bring about change?*

CHAPTER EIGHT

WHO'S THE CHAMPION AGAIN?

A message that is not constantly repeated loses its sway and becomes yet another well-meaning management suggestion rather than an executive-level decree. Company leaders must be steadfast in their evangelizing efforts to bring planning efforts into reality.

> *While it's imperative that the rank-and-file see senior leaders waving the flag and leading the charge toward a better tomorrow, senior leaders simply will not have the interaction with company staff—at least not to the degree necessary—that's required to ensure the planning efforts are worked daily.*

Often, management falls into the trap of chasing the next shiny object. In doing so, they bombard employees with a myriad of different messages to the point where they are suborned into inaction.

While it's imperative that the rank-and-file see senior leaders waving the flag and leading the charge toward a better tomorrow, senior leaders simply will not have the interaction with company staff—at least not to the degree necessary—that's required to ensure the planning efforts are worked daily. Running the company and keeping peer-level colleagues on the same page can be like herding cats and is more than a full-time job in and of itself. While it would be great for senior leaders to hit the pavement and personally work the change effort, you simply do not have the time to directly engage with corporate staff, day in and day out.

A major *Forbes* study regarding trends in human capital found that companies across the world are finding it increasingly difficult to meaningfully engage with the modern workforce of the twenty-first century. In fact, the results are pretty dismal. Only 13% of employees across 2,500 organizations across the world felt that they are actively engaged by their supervisors (much less senior leaders) at work. And it gets worse, as more than a quarter of these employees complain that the engagement epidemic is so bad, they're likely to spread negativity to others.[69]

This problem is orders of magnitude more severe when considering the fraction of time that employees are walked through strategic initiatives as the majority of managers only engage employees for daily task management, if even that, as this study shows.

Pass the Buck—and the Baton

Rather than rely on senior leaders to convey the message of strategic change, you need to assign a group of executives and a series of lower-level managers below them who can gauge the daily business of bringing about strategic initiatives on a personal level with line-level staff.

These lower-ranking executives and managers should be given the authority to broker disagreements across divisions as business planning is worked. In addition, this group of executives and middle managers, together with the staff-level series of employees needed to bring about strategic initiatives, needs to be accountable for the set of objectives (e.g., a 5% increase in market share in the next quarter) and metrics (e.g., leading measures such as the number of working groups aimed at bringing about that increase in market share, etc.) necessary for the company to achieve the end result.

The US Navy, like myriad other public- and private-sector organizations, has been eyewitness and benefactor of what can happen when senior leaders push strategy and strategic planning down to line-level staff members. Once denigrated as the poorest performer of the Navy's nuclear-class submarines, the USS *Santa Fe* was in need of a significant course correction. As one of America's premier weapons and first line of defense against a nuclear threat, the *Santa Fe* was in danger of dipping below a performance level that might, under certain scenarios, place America's security at risk.

The knee-jerk reaction of most organizations and senior leaders would involve placing all command-and-control decision-making authority in one centralized figure. Having served in the military, I am confident the crew aboard the USS *Santa Fe* was also certain the ramifications of their poor performance would mean they would have to follow every word that the new captain of the ship, David Marquet, would utter.

However, leaving the "decision-making" to senior leaders is often a palliative treatment for issues that only line-level staff can often remedy. Captain Marquet's approach elucidates the need for executives to trust their employees in bringing about improvements to entrenched issues, which often come with a deep history.

In his contrarian approach, Captain Marquet imbued his submarine crew with the autonomy and authority to make those decisions that would bring about an almost miraculous turnaround in the ship's poor performance. Shortly after instituting this, the USS *Santa Fe* began to garner awards from the US Navy for evaluation scores and crew retention that would last well beyond Marquet's time as captain of the ship.[70]

Executives at companies such as Netflix, who have garnered so much success that they have become household names, pride themselves in decentralized decision-making. Reed Hastings, former CEO of Netflix, proudly asserts, "I pride myself in making as few decisions as possible in a quarter. Sometimes I can go a whole quarter without making any decisions."[71]

By pushing down decision-making to the corporate workforce, Netflix has quickly been able to pivot its direction based on the ebbs and flows of the environment around them for over two decades. Initially, Netflix provided DVD rentals to initial customers. By changing their business model to emphasize streaming services instead of physical DVD rentals, they singlehandedly transformed the entertainment industry. Providing teams with the autonomy to make decisions at the lowest levels possible and allowing them the room to learn from their mistakes has definitely paid off for Netflix—to the tune of approximately $20 billion.[72]

We Cannot Lead a Horse to Water . . . But If We Could . . .

The somewhat counterintuitive approach of pushing decision-making down might not be a leadership panacea that will solve all issues of organizational life. It does, however, offer a rapid-fire capability that companies can use in this time of dynamic change. Unfortunately, in a study recently launched across over 300 corporate leaders, only about 42 senior leaders asserted that decisions are pushed down to those employees who have the pulse of the problem.[73] This is rather unfortunate. The other 250+ senior leaders in this survey employ a decision-making model that creates headwinds that kill the momentum and escape velocity needed for their companies to act on information they need to navigate to reach the shores of profitability and growth.

The somewhat counterintuitive approach of pushing decision-making down might not be a leadership panacea that will solve all issues of organizational life. It does, however, offer a rapid-fire capability that companies can use in this time of dynamic change.

Be the Broker

When emphasizing the importance of pushing decision-making down to those employees closest to the pulse of the problem, we also need to be clear that accountability for the improved future condition still rests squarely on the shoulders of senior leaders. But how exactly can senior leaders strike the balance of providing autonomy to the rank-and-file while keeping accountability for the end result?

One of the most effective means of doing so is by taking on the role of a broker. This means senior leaders will only get involved in direct decision-making when their rank is required to break any stalemates that might be created between two (usually) equally ranked teams of people (e.g., divisions, branches, regions, etc., whose decision-makers are of equal authority) and the decision with which they are grappling.

For example, one division might vehemently believe the best way to achieve operational efficiencies is via consolidation of all similar divisions beneath them, while the other division might doggedly believe the best way to achieve operational efficiencies is via complete and tailored segregation, reporting chains, responsibilities, and their own budget for each division. If the leads of each division are equal in seniority and authority, this argument can take on a life of its own. That is unless someone with more authority over each group can weigh in and break the stalemate by making the decision on how both divisions should approach the objective to gain operational efficiencies.

This is exactly the situation in which I squarely found myself when trying to bring about a major shift across a diverse and geographically separated workforce. I needed to change the dismal future outlook of exponentially rising costs coming from antiquated equipment, an aging work force that was retiring, labor union unrest, and an approach to accomplishing the mission at hand that had not changed in decades! The organization was grappling with the desire to change culture and the definition of what the group was in the business of doing, but became embroiled in the tug-of-war over whose ideas would be implemented.

However, the solution is *not* to bring the impasse to the executive responsible for both divisions, but rather to one who can see the situation holistically, with a fresh perspective and without bias. This should be someone who is willing and able to make the tough call, regardless of how unpopular that call might be with employees and executives alike.

Xerox has been at the forefront of technical solutions for everyday businesses since 1906. But when the business environment started turning cold from fears of recession, increasing interest rates, and rampant inflation in early 2023, CEO Steve Bandrowczak knew he had to get in front of the mounting dilemma. Instead of a command-and-control approach to combat the impending storm, he relied on the company's cultural resiliency to innovate solutions that will help it navigate the economic crisis. He asked his leadership to think like consumers and employ new and advantageous technology through the venue of culture rather than technology adoption alone.

Most of all, he stood his ground, instilled confidence across the rank-and-file, and let them roll up their sleeves and get to work. Bandrowczak asserted, "When you're leading a large group and you get hit with economic challenges, or supply chain challenges, or whatever, everybody in the company is looking to you as a leader for calm. They're looking for you to not have fear and show the way forward."[74]

Time Does Not Equal Money

Time and worry are directly proportional: the more time it takes for leaders to act, the more angst and consternation build among the rank-and-file. Conversely, time and momentum are inversely proportional: The more time decisions about the strategic direction of the firm lay in wait, the more the momentum for change deteriorates. However, the relationship here is not just inversely proportional—it's *exponentially* inversely proportional. For every week that passes by without the mention of the strategic initiative at hand, the enthusiasm for the initiative drops disproportionately, until one day it gets to the point of no return. It's at this point that there's almost nothing senior leaders can do to reinvigorate employees' inspiration to bring about change.

Company employees need to see their leadership actively working the strategic vision of the company, or the energy for change will be drowned out by fears and employee uncertainty about the true commitment to the visionary initiative on the part of company leaders—not to mention the barrage of everyday corporate life. This is the reason the deterioration mentioned earlier expands exponentially with each passing day.

The overwhelming majority of companies fail to make their strategic priorities visible. In fact, in a study recently undertaken across 124 large companies, less than 35 of them had middle managers who had a clue what those strategic goals were on any given day.[75] If the picture for middle managers' cognizance of strategy is so dismal, rank-and-file employees have no chance of even throwing their hat in the ring when it comes to the fight to bring about strategic plans.

Bottoms Up

The CEO of what was then a fledgling Brazilian beer brewer known as Companhia Cervejaria Brahma had no idea that his most impactful endeavor at the struggling local beer brewery would be his approach to the strategic goal-setting process.

Having been a stock market trader for a large portion of his career, Marcel Telles was used to the transparency of the exchange floor, and he had an inkling that transparency at Companhia Cervejaria Brahma could turn the tide. Telles went right to work and tore down stove pipes and cubicle walls. He made it a habit to post the company's strategic goals and the company's performance against those benchmarks in an open forum where all employees—regardless of rank—could see where the company stood against them at any point in time.

The company is now known as AB InBev and is now *the* most profitable beer maker in the world. While shedding the original company name, Telles has continued to prioritize the transparency of all corporate goals and performance toward them, warts and all, for all employees to see.[76]

Making sure to push down goal-setting and implementation authority to those employees with the pulse on the problem is critical. However, senior leaders must then follow up by trumpeting those resulting strategic goals—and the organization's progress in meeting those goals—at every potential opportunity. Company leaders must use their platform to voice these goals so that the entire organization receives the same message, time and time again.

Questions to Consider

- *Are you constantly shifting focus? Or, are you steadfast in your resolve to bring about corporate strategy into reality?*
- *Do you trust your employees with the ability to identify the best solution to the problems plaguing your company?*
- *When was the last time you made yourself available to listen to disagreements among major divisions about the way to bring about corporate strategy?*
- *Do employees have a means of knowing how the company, by appropriate divisions, is performing relative to strategic goals?*

CHAPTER NINE

BOILING IT DOWN

Forget What You Thought You Knew About Strategy

The old, archaic, go-through-the-motion process of setting a strategy, going on autopilot, and visiting that years-old strategy—only to revise it and move on—is costing you market share, customer loyalty, employee turnover, and motivation.

> *The real value in strategy is the sheer act of setting it in a way that is inclusive, engaging, optimistic, and challenges the status quo. It's about addressing the painful, perhaps borderline embarrassing issues the company is facing and knocking them down one-by-one.*

There is absolutely nothing exciting about setting or revising a strategy for the purpose of writing down future goals and objectives, then putting it on the shelf to collect dust while the company continues to operate as usual. The real value in strategy is the sheer act of setting it in a way that is inclusive, engaging, optimistic, and challenges the status quo. It's about addressing the painful, perhaps borderline embarrassing issues the company is facing and knocking them down one-by-one.

Moreover, top leadership needs to prioritize the organization's ability to set strategy in a dynamic, high-energy, fast-paced battle rhythm that reinforces the firm's ability to pivot quickly and make quick and constant course corrections along the way.

Think Less

Planning for the future is also an act of futility if your organization is not positioned, provisioned, and resourced to take immediate action on the plan that's been laid out.

Well-laid plans are great, but they quickly become that inert, sometimes obtrusive paper weight that really serves no purpose—other than getting a kick out of glancing at it by people passing by your desk. It's paramount first to tally the ability of your company to pounce on the strategy before it's even laid out, rather than to expend valuable time creating a plan that will just age badly on the shelf like a carton of milk. Plans are nothing without enough escape velocity to accelerate the group out of the status quo, to get people out of their proverbial seats, and leaping into immediate action.

What's more, plans that are crafted without the momentum needed to fully be enacted—even in an expert fashion—leave the company in a much worse position than if the plan were not created at all. Strategic roadmaps that are shelved only serve as reminders to employees that these plans are mere paper exercises, drafted by executives and senior leaders in an ivory tower as part of their obligatory responsibilities and not really meant to be acted upon or even considered.

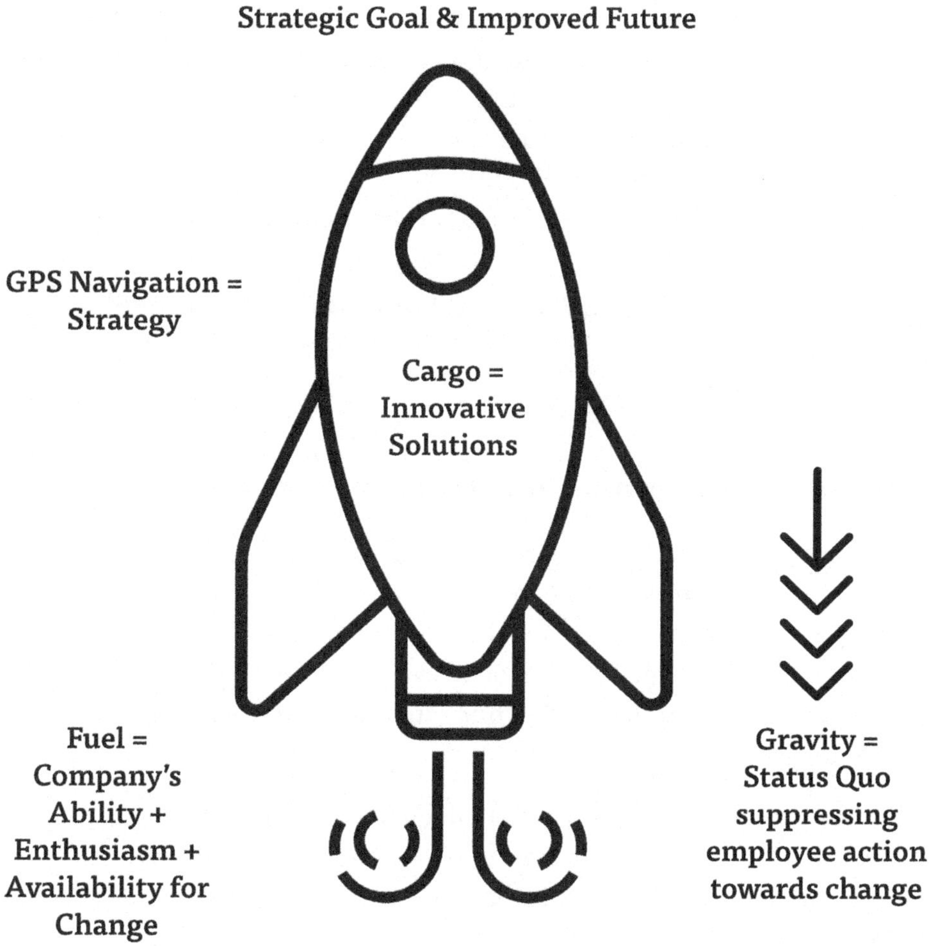

Get Lean, Mean, and Empower the Team

The risks, dynamics, and breakneck pace of change in today's environment mean you need less centralized decision-making, less executive hand-holding, and more of the people that are at the crux of the issues and the forefront of your customer interaction at the helm of strategic formulation and implementation. Given the strategic role technology now plays in any company's array of capabilities, technology experts have to be part of the strategic team. Their input must be consistently solicited and earnestly digested if any company hopes to remain competitive in our technology-led landscape.

Add to that the dire need for a dedicated, full-time project management team to lead the implementation of strategic change if those strategic plans are to be followed consistently, robustly, professionally, and in a manner that mitigates risks and manages stakeholder groups along the way. Handing over the task of implementation to employees or senior leaders who are already bogged down with the tasks of everyday operations, managing the company, or handling their primary job is a recipe for disaster at worst and a precondition for lackluster results at best.

Become the Champion You Are Destined to Be

Once strategic plans are created, you must constantly and consistently champion the message, the effort, and the results of implementation. However, this sponsorship also needs to be shouldered by lower-level executives, middle management, and employees closest to the areas where change or improvement are most needed.

The messaging of the strategy itself should be pushed as far down as possible so that it can be done by those most capable of bringing about change at the lowest levels possible and so that the effort can maintain a strong level of momentum and escape velocity to make positive change possible.

Last But Not Least of All—It's What You Become that Is the Real Destination

Above all the benefits of the strategic planning and implementation effort is the transformative power this process possesses to evolve the organization to enable the vision of what the company should become. This is really the central question that strategy needs to consider as it helps forge the course of how to get to that end-game destination.

At the end of the day, the burden of leadership is to shape the framework and cornerstone of what the company needs to become. This is the set of tangible and intangible identities that the organization is striving to become—the set of character traits, values, and culture that embodies, or should embody, and cuts to the core of what the enterprise is all about. It's our job as senior leaders to build this bedrock.

> *At the end of the day, the burden of leadership is to shape the framework and cornerstone of what the company needs to become. This is the set of tangible and intangible identities that the organization is striving to become—the set of character traits, values, and culture that embodies, or should embody, and cuts to the core of what the enterprise is all about.*

It's then within this framework and architecture that strategic planning charts the course, with the utmost consideration that the roadmap being charted aligns to that anchor point. Leadership needs to invest in building this bedrock and framework in laying out the pathway that leads the company to what it should become. Unfortunately, there are far too many organizations that simply go through the motions when it comes to forming company identity and culture. This haphazard approach inevitably leads the business to that perilous condition of being tossed around by every whim, fear, and wince caused by the constant ebb and flow of the marketplace.

Are you taking your company to new heights? More importantly, do your employees know what you are trying to become in the process?

Here's to your arrival at your envisioned destination!

ACKNOWLEDGMENTS

I owe all of what I have learned over the course of so many years to the mentors, mentees, managers, colleagues, and friends with whom I've been blessed to cross paths:

Glenn Ballentine and Ron Arsenault, two retired Air Force senior NCOs who early on in my career taught me to tackle any undertaking with accountability and leadership at all costs.

Steve Koeneker, a world-class engineer, leader, and retired Air Force officer who embodies all the values of work ethic, ingenuity, and mentorship that I have come to admire. Steve and I worked countless hours and late nights over several years forming the strategy and execution plan of a successful multibillion change effort for a very large government organization. Steve was also monumental in helping launch our consulting business.

Kerry Bauerschmidt, an exemplary supervisor and brilliant senior systems engineer who taught me volumes about systems integration, leadership, and gave me the opportunity to lead teams of brilliant technical experts. Like Steve, Kerry was also instrumental in launching New Beacon Consulting.

My friend, business partner, and fellow Air Force veteran, Matt Eucalitto, has the ability to think calmly under pressure. His unwavering commitment to our growth helps propel our practice forward.

Ben Foote, whose optimism, entrepreneurial acumen, and leadership ability taught me volumes and made my job as mentor and supervisor during the first couple of years of his career a fantastic learning opportunity. Ben's encouragement led me to take the plunge in launching our business and writing this book.

Alan Weiss, one of the absolute best consultants of his time, who emboldened me to write this book and provide value to all of the myriad of organizations stand to benefit from my experiences in leadership, strategy, and change management.

Linda Popky, Jenn LeBlanc, and Emily Bouchard, whose expertise in marketing, brand building, and website design have provided volumes of inestimable guidance in building our brand.

All of the officers, enlisted men and women, civil servants, fellow contractors, and leaders with whom I have had the pleasure of working and serving throughout these past 20+ years—your dedication, sacrifice, and work ethic make the impossible, possible. Thank you all.

Finally, my wife, Rachelle, who constantly personifies the value of pulling out all the stops to get those endeavors that are as daunting as they are worthwhile. Your work ethic and dedication inspire me.

ABOUT THE AUTHOR

Robert Aguilar is the founder and CEO of New Beacon Consulting Group. He has over 20 years of experience in program management, systems engineering, and strategic change consulting across multiple industries. Robert started his career as an Air Force acquisition officer. After multiple leadership positions, he transitioned to roles in strategic leadership. In this capacity, he has led myriad strategy, change management, and organizational development efforts worth over $2.5 billion to his clients.

Robert holds an MBA from the Marshall School of Business at the University of Southern California with an emphasis in corporate strategy and consulting and a BA in business economics from California State University, Fullerton.

A native of Southern California, Robert loves to be immersed in the vast multicultural dynamic that is characteristic of the Southern California lifestyle.

Robert enjoys mountain biking, skiing, piloting single-engine aircraft, building radio control cars and is, to his knowledge, the only left-handed person brave enough to use a fountain pen.

NOTES

[1]https://www.forbes.com/sites/businessreporter/2020/01/27/what-will-the-future-of-work-look-like-a-view-from-2030/amp/.

[2]https://www.businessinsider.com/rise-and-fall-of-blockbuster.

[3]https://strategyand.pwc.com/gx/en/unique-solutions/capabilities-driven-strategy/approach/research-motivation.html.

[4]https://fortune.com/2030/04/20/ikea-17-more-locations-us-expansion/amp.

[5] https://hbr.org/2022/06/4-common-reasons-strategies-fail.

[6]https://www.ey.com/en_us/strategy/four-ways-to-rethink-how-you-develop-strategy.

[7]https://news.harvard.edu/gazette/story/2010/11/wandering-mind-not-a-happy-mind/.

[8]https://amp.cnn.com/cnn/2020/08/10/business/amazon.

[9]https://www.axios.com/2019/06/27/amazon-shipping-chart-fedex-ups-usps.

[10]https://www.mckinsey.com/~/media/mckinsey/business%20functions/marketing%20and%20sales/our%20insights/mindset%20to%20action%20imperatives%20for%20growth/mindset-to-action-imperatives-for-growth.pdf.

[11]https://www.forbes.com/sites/forbeslacouncil/2019/01/28/the-most-dangerous-phrase-in-business-weve-always-done-it-this-way/.

[12]https://hbr.org/2022/06/4-common-reasons-strategies-fail.

[13]https://fortune.com/2020/07/15/chipotle-hiring-coronavirus-workers-drive-thru-mobile-orders-covid-19/.

[14]https://haslamgradprograms.utk.edu/2022/11/22/why-strategic-leadership-skills-are-critical-in-executive-level-roles/.

[15]https://www.clearpointstrategy.com/blog/strategic-planning-statistics.

[16]https://lifeclub.org/books/make-change-work-for-you-scott-steinberg-review-summary.

[17]https://www.sdcexec.com/sourcing-procurement/article/20985884/ihs-inc-what-are-late-product-launches-really-costing-you.

[18]https://fortune.com/2022/11/07/ibm-america-must-invest-new-model-innovation-silicon-valley-chips-semiconductors-computing-tech/.

[19]https://investors.micron.com/news-releases/news-release-details/micron-announces-historic-investment-100-billion-build-megafab#.

[20]https://www.wolfspeed.com/company/news-events/news/wolfspeed-selects-north-carolina-for-worlds-largest-silicon-carbide-materials-facility/.

[21]https://voicesofdemocracy.umd.edu/roosevelt-strenuous-life-1899-speech-text/.

[22]https://www.lendingtree.com/business/small/failure-rate/.

[23]https://hbr.org/2022/08/in-uncertain-times-the-best-strategy-is-adaptability.

[24]https://hbr.org/1996/11/the-human-side-of-management.

[25]https://www.bcg.com/publications/most-innovative-companies-historical-rankings.

[26]https://hbr.org/2020/04/if-youre-burning-out-carve-a-new-path.

[27]https://blog.adobe.com/en/publish/2022/08/31/adobe-receives-recognition-as-top-company-that-cares-for-employees-their-communities.

[28]https://www.businessinsider.com/gamestop-worlds-biggest-video-game-retailer-decline-explained-2019-7.

[29]https://airandspace.si.edu/stories/editorial/remembering-tom-wolfe-and-right-stuff.

[30]https://strategosinc.com/RESOURCES/04-Lean_History/harley-davidson.htm.

[31] https://www.forbes.com/sites/jsimms/2021/09/09/japans-olympus-aims-to-become-global-medtech-leader-after-exiting-cameras/.

[32]https://www.fool.com/investing/2023/08/24/peloton-woes-stock-hits-new-low-can-stock-rebound/.

[33]https://www.gartner.com/en/human-resources/insights/organizational-change-management.

[34]https://hbr.org/1995/05/leading-change-why-transformation-efforts-fail-2

[35]https://finance.yahoo.com/news/enphase-energy-enph-q4-earnings-135101058.html.

[36]https://forbes.com%2Fsites%2Fforbestechcouncil%2F2023%2F03%2F28%2Fgen-z-striking-the-balance-between-job-flexibility-and-job-security.

[37]https://www.nytimes.com/2023/05/14/business/economy/wealth-generations.html.

[38]https://www.thinkindependent.com.au/aint-dont-know-gets-trouble/.

[39]https://www.mckinsey.com/~/media/mckinsey/business%20functions/people%20and%20organizational%20performance/our%20insights/the%20state%20of%20organizations%202023/the-state-of-organizations-2023.pdf.

[40]https://www.logicgate.com/blog/logicgate-founders-look-back-on-the-last-7-years/.

[41]https://westword.com/news/crocs-colorado-company-twentieth-anniversary-15261577

[42]https://www.techtarget.com/searchcloudcomputing/news/252529449/Latest-Google-Cloud-AI-shines-spotlight-on-retail-automation.

[43]https://www.defense.gov/News/News-Stories/Article/Article/3058028/digital-transformation-ai-important-in-keeping-battlefield-edge-leaders-say/.

[44]https://news.walgreens.com/press-center/walgreens-boots-alliance-makes-52-billion-investment-in-villagemd-to-deliver-value-based-primary-care-to-communities-across-america.htm.

[45]https://www.boozallen.com/insights/digital-twin/building-dods-largest-ever-digital-twin-of-its-kind.html.

[46]https://www.oprah.com/oprahshow/big-ideas-big-bucks/all.

[47]https://www.prnewswire.com/news-releases/mcloud-and-google-cloud-partner-to-launch-trio-of-sustainability-apps-aimed-at-curbing-carbon-emissions-worldwide-301661009.html.

[48]https://hbr.org/2021/05/identify-and-hire-lifelong-learners.

[49]https://hbr.org/2022/11/what-really-makes-toyotas-production-system-resilient.

[50]https://www.forbes.com/sites/tracybrower/2022/11/06/70-arent-prepared-for-the-future-of-work-demands-for-upskilling-surge/.

[51]https://www2.deloitte.com/content/dam/Deloitte/us/Documents/technology-media-telecommunications/us-tmt-22-deloitte-technology-fast-500-ranking-list.pdf.

[52]https://www.shrm.org/hr-today/news/hr-magazine/winter2021/pages/upskilling-as-an-equalizer-ray-mabus/.

[53]https://hbr.org/2022/11/linkedin-ceo-ryan-roslansky-skills-not-degrees-matter-most-in-hiring.

[54]https://hmgstrategy.com/press-releases/cio-leadership-hmg-strategy-announces-record-growth-publishes-distinctive-2023-events-calendar-for-forward-thinking-global-tech-leaders/.

[55]https://hospitalityinsights.ehl.edu/food-trucks-disrupting-fb-industry.

[56]https://www.imeche.org/news/news-article/uncrewed-rocket-explosions-part-of-progress-in-fast-moving-modern-space-industry.

[57]https://www.icmrindia.org/casestudies/catalogue/Operations/Ford%20Production%20System-Operations%20Management%20Case%20Studies.htm.

[58]https://www.mullenusa.com/mullen-five.

[59]https://www.cnbc.com/2022/03/02/fanatics-hits-27-billion-in-new-funding-adds-blackrock-michael-dell.html#:~:text=Michael%20Rubin%27s%20Fanatics%20has%20raised,as%20well%20as%20existing%20investors.

[60]https://www.cnbc.com/2022/04/11/fanatics-aims-to-be-100-billion-company.html.

[61]https://www.businessinsider.com/large-companies-best-ceos-comparably-2020-12.

[62]https://www.6sigma.us/kaizen/trader-joes-kaizen-marriage-made-heaven/.

[63]https://www.salesforce.com/uk/company/our-story/.

[64]https://fourweekmba.com/nike-vision-statement-mission-statement/.

[65]https://startuptalky.com/blockbuster-its-rise-and-fall/.

[66]https://www.cnbc.com/2022/07/31/google-ceo-to-employees-productivity-and-focus-must-improve.html.

[67]https://about.google/intl/en-GB/commitments/.

[68]https://www.marketingweek.com/pg-prioritise-investment-over-bottom-line/.

[69]https://www.forbes.com/sites/joshbersin/2014/03/15/why-companies-fail-to-engage-todays-workforce-the-overwhelmed-employee/?sh=3f2672654726.

[70]https://web.nps.edu/Images/Docs/JAN13%20InReview.pdf.

[71]https://www.forbes.com/sites/danpontefract/2019/02/04/the-netflix-decision-making-model-is-why-theyre-so-successful/?sh=42a5705173bc.

[72]https://www.forbes.com/sites/danpontefract/2019/02/04/the-netflix-decision-making-model-is-why-theyre-so-successful/?sh=4ef7c72973bc.

[73]https://hbr.org/2018/07/how-ceos-manage-time.

[74]https://www.businessroundtable.org/about-us/members/steven-bandrowczak-chief-executive-officer-xerox-holdings-corporation.

[75]https://sloanreview.mit.edu/article/no-one-knows-your-strategy-not-even-your-top-leaders/.

[76]https://www.statista.com/statistics/257670/sales-of-the-leading-beer-companies-worldwide/#:~:text=Sales%20of%20the%20leading%20beer%20companies%20worldwide%202023&text=Anheuser%2DBusch%20InBev%20was%20the,sales%20of%2030.2%20billion%20dollars.

Made in the USA
Las Vegas, NV
21 November 2024

11852331R00056